Women Were Pirates, Too

Pirates,
Too

C. T. Anthony

Piracy Is Prohibited!

Dear reader, please note that all rights to the content of this book are reserved. No part of this work may be reproduced or used in any form or by any means—graphic, electronic, or mechanical, including photocopying or information storage and retrieval systems—without written permission from the publisher. The scanning, uploading and distribution of this book or any part thereof via the Internet or via any other means without the permission of the publisher is illegal and punishable by law. Please purchase only authorized editions and do not participate in or encourage the electronic piracy of copyrighted materials.

"Schiffer," "Schiffer Publishing Ltd. & Design," and the "Design of pen and ink well" are registered trademarks of Schiffer Publishing Ltd.

Your input and corrections, in writing, are most welcome regarding this presentation. Further, we are always looking for people to write books on new and related subjects. If you have an idea for a book please contact us at the above address.

Copyright © 2006
by Schiffer Publishing, Ltd.

Library of Congress Control Number:
2006920775

Type set in Aldine 721 BT

ISBN: 0-7643-2492-6
Printed in China

Published by Schiffer Publishing Ltd.
4880 Lower Valley Road
Atglen, PA 19310
Phone: (610) 593-1777
Fax: (610) 593-2002
E-mail: Info@schifferbooks.com
www.schifferbooks.com

This book may be purchased from the publisher. Include $3.95 for shipping. Please try your bookstore first.

Write for a free catalog.

In Europe, Schiffer books are distributed by Bushwood Books
6 Marksbury Ave.
Kew Gardens
Surrey TW9 4JF England
Phone: 44 (0) 20 8392-8585
Fax: 44 (0) 20 8392-9876
E-mail: info@bushwoodbooks.co.uk
Website: www.bushwoodbooks.co.uk

Postage is free in the U.K., Europe, airmail at cost.

Table of Contents

Introduction

Before nations organized coast guard patrols and hammered out agreements governing coastal and international waters, might was right on the high seas. A pirate ship that could out-man and out-gun another made free use of the other's cargo, personnel, and even the ship itself if it suited the sackers. Nor were pirates always considered the bad guys. England, for one, encouraged Privateers to sack Spanish ships, and other European nations likewise worked to forcefully extract some of the wealth that Spanish ships were hauling home from closely guarded ports in the New World.

Piracy often operated in the interests of enriching monarchs and warlords, and coastal countries around the world took various liberties with whatever vessels might pass nearby. As Colonel John Biddulph wrote, by the turn of the 20th century, people were already forgetting "the tremendous risks and difficulties under which (our forefathers' . . .) trade was maintained, the losses that were suffered, and the dangers that were run . . . from the moment they left the English Channel. The privations and dangers of the voyage to India were alone sufficient to deter all but the hardiest spirits, and the debt we owe to those who, by painful effort, won a footing for our Indian trade, is deserving of more recognition than it has received.

"Scurvy, shortness of water, and mutinous crews were to be reckoned on in every voyage; navigation was not a science but a matter of rule and thumb, and shipwreck was frequent; while every coast was inhospitable. It is difficult to realize, in these days, what a terrible scourge piracy was . . . two hundred years ago. A ship was never safe from attack, with the chance of slavery or a cruel death to crew and passengers. From Finisterre to Cape Verde the Moorish pirates made the seas unsafe, sometimes venturing into the mouth of the Channel to make a capture. Farther south, every watering-place on the African coast was infested by the English and French pirates who had their headquarters in the West Indies. From the Cape of Good Hope to the head of the Persian Gulf, from Cape Comorin to Sumatra, every coast was beset by English, French, Dutch, Danish, Portuguese, Arab, Malay, or other local pirates."

In the Americas, pirates diligently worked the coasts, from the warm Caribbean waters to the ports of New England, piracy was a ever-present danger to merchant and seaman alike.

"There was no peace on the ocean. The sea was a vast No Man's domain, where every man might take his prey. Law and order stopped short at low-water mark. The principle that traders might claim protection and vengeance for their wrongs from their country, had not yet been recognized, and they sailed the seas at their own risk. Before the close of the seventeenth century the buccaneers had passed away, but their depredations, in pursuit of what they called "free trade," were of a different nature from those of the pirates who succeeded them. Buccaneer exploits were confined to the Spanish main, where they ravaged and burnt Spanish settlements on the Atlantic and Pacific coasts, moving with large forces by sea and land. According to Esquemeling, Morgan sailed on his expedition against Panama with thirty-seven sail and two thousand fighting men, besides mariners and boys," Biddulph wrote. "But the Spanish alone were the objects of their attack. So long as Spain claimed a monopoly of South American trade, it was the business of Spain alone to keep the marauders away; other Governments were not disposed to assist her. Hardly had the last of the buccaneers disappeared from the Western seas, when a more lawless race of rovers appeared, extending their operations into the Indian Ocean, acting generally in single ships, plundering vessels of every nationality, though seldom attacking places on shore.

"Of these men, chiefly English, the most notorious were Teach (Blackbeard), Every, Kidd, Roberts, England, and Tew; but there were many others less known to fame, who helped almost to extinguish trade between Europe, America, and the East. Some idea of the enormous losses caused by them may be gathered from the fact that Bartholomew Roberts alone was credited with the destruction of four hundred trading vessels in three years. In a single day he captured eleven vessels, English, French, and Portuguese, on the African coast."

Biddulph related that pirates, "whatever their nationality might chance to be," were generally "courageous rascals and splendid seamen, who, with their large crews, handled their ships better than any merchantmen could do. When a pirate ship was cast away on a desolate coast, they built themselves another; the spirit of the sea was in their veins; whether building and rigging a ship, or sailing and fighting her, they could do everything that the most skillful seamen of the age could do. As was said half a century later of La Bourdonnais, himself a true corsair in spirit, their knowledge in mechanics rendered them capable of building a ship from the keel; their skill in navigation, of conducting her to any part of the globe; and their courage, of fighting against any equal force.

"Their lives were a continual alternation between idleness and extreme toil, riotous debauchery and great privation, prolonged monotony and days of great excitement and adventure. At one moment they were reveling in unlimited rum, and gambling for handfuls of gold and diamonds; at another, half starving for food and reduced to a pint of water

6

a day under a tropical sun. Yet the attractions of the life were so great that men of good position took to piracy. . . Even women, like Anne Bonny and Mary Read, turned pirates and handled sword and pistol. Desperate, reckless, and lawless, they were filled with the spirit of adventure."

Yet how did two such women manage to operate as equals in a culture so given to violence, often against women? Moreover, to make such a leap in gender roles during a time when life was so cramped, unwholesome and uncomfortable aboard the kind of fast-sailing vessel pirates preferred. Such a life was not only considered improper for a "delicate" woman, it was considered unlucky to have a female aboard. Given to superstitions, and given that their lives were ruled by the unpredictable tempests of Mother Nature, sailors shared a common belief that women brought bad luck to sailing vessels. Still, there are many recorded stories of women disguising themselves and securing positions upon sailing ships, according to David Cordingly, a contemporary scholar of pirate history and culture. "The history of the Royal Navy and the merchant service is littered with examples of women who successfully dressed as men and worked alongside them for years without being discovered," he wrote in *Under the Black Flag*.

Cordingly posits that women may have successfully disguised themselves as young men, who were often brought on board to do the bulk of the work. If she was comfortable climbing into the rigging, and proved herself equal to the men on board, they might never have reason to question her.

Most of the stories in this book are about women who openly operated as such, acting as leaders and equals among men and earning their respect without any pretenses about being manly themselves. But we will start off with two women who typified the life of the Caribbean pirate, so much in vogue now with recent Hollywood releases. Mary Read somehow entered the life of pirate while disguised as a man, while Anne Bonney came aboard as a pirate's lover. By coincidence they found each other out, though their disguises had presumably fooled all the others on board.

Anne Bonney and Mary Read

The most famous female pirates were Anne Bonney and Mary Read, two women captured at the end of the pirate's rule over the balmy dominions of the Caribbean. Their account first came to light in a book published by a Captain Charles Johnson in 1724, *A General History of the Robberies & Murders of the Most Notorious Pirates*, and recounted in numerous pirate tomes since, including the oft reprinted *Pirate's Own Book*, first published by the Marine Research Society, 1924. Bonney and Read were captured in the company of a John Rackam, a notorious pirate who skirted both sides of the law, working for a time within the legal realms of privateering, but crossing over into illegal pursuits. Bonney is known to have left her lawful husband to accompany him on his exploits, and fought by his side. How Mary Read came to be in their company is less clear. As the story relates, her gender was only revealed when Bonney pursued her as a love interest, and the jealous John Rackam was admitted to their confidence lest he challenge Mary in a man-to-man duel.

In order to preserve the skeletal facts accurately, they are here presented here in nearly verbatim form, from the original 1724 account:

Captain John Rackam

John Rackam merits space in this book as the captain caught with two women among the crew of his pirate ship in 1720. Anne Bonney joined him, deserting her husband and engaging as an ardent participant aboard an outlaw ship.

Rackam's recorded piratical career begins with his role as quartermaster to Captain Charles Vane, a notorious pirate whose exploits were widespread, and whose acquaintances included the notorious Blackbeard. Rackam rose in rank through a rebellion against Vane, accusing him of cowardice for refusing to board a French man-of-war. Rackam was voted captain of the division that remained in Vane's brigantine and on November 24, 1718, the first day of his command, he plundered several vessels in the Caribbean.

When Captain Woods Rogers arrived as the new Governor of the island of Providence, he brought with him the British King's pardon for pirates ready to surrender, and a determination to hunt down those who would not. Rackam was among the latter. Escaping narrowly from harbor, Rackam bid defiance to the mercy that was offered.

Subsequently, he led a doomed life of small-time piracy, with a diminished crew operating in waters increasingly more dangerous for lawless seamen. Rackam kept a little kind of a family in Cuba, and his crew stayed there for a while, "living ashore with their Delilahs, till their money and provisions were expended, and they concluded it time to look out for more," Johnson wrote. Their vessel repaired, they were making ready to put to sea when a Spanish Guarda de Costa came in with a small English sloop, which she had taken as an interloper on the coast. The Spanish guard-ship attacked the pirate, but Rackam being close in behind a little island, she could do but little execution where she lay. The Spanish ship therefore blocked the channel that evening, in order to make sure of Rackam's capture the next morning.

Finding his case desperate, Rackam packed his crew into a small boat in the dead of night, heavily armed, and they stealthily rowed their way to the Spaniard's first prize, the English sloop, lying for better security close to land between the little island and the Main. Rackam's crew boarded the sloop without being discovered, and once in charge told the Spaniards that if they spoke a word, or made the least noise, they were all dead men. Thus Rackam affected his escape.

Future conquests were meager, with booty that included nets forced from fishermen and cattle wrested from islanders. In the French part of Hispaniola, they found two or three Frenchmen by the waterside, hunting wild hogs in the evening. The Frenchmen came on board, whether by consent or compulsion is not certainly known. In Jamaica, on the north coast near Porto Maria Bay, they took a schooner, Thomas Spenlow, master, it being then the 19th of October. The next day Rackam seeing a sloop in Dry Harbour Bay, stood in and fired a gun; the men all ran ashore, and he took the sloop and lading; but when those ashore found that they were pirates, they hailed the sloop, and let them know they were all willing to come on board.

Rackam's coasting the island in this manner proved fatal to him; for intelligence of his expedition soon came to Governor Rogers. A sloop was immediately fitted out, and sent round the island in quest of him, commanded by Captain Barnet, and manned with a good number of hands. Rackam, rounding the island, and drawing round the western point, called Point Negril, saw a small boat, which, at the sight of the sloop, ran ashore and landed her men. Discovering that they were Englishmen, Rackam's crew invited the small crew onboard for a drink. Accordingly, the company, in an evil hour, came all aboard of the pirate, consisting of nine persons; they were armed with muskets and cutlasses, but what was their real design in so doing we will not pretend to say. They had no sooner laid down their arms and taken up their pipes, than Barnet's sloop, which was in pursuit of Rackam's, came in sight.

The pirates, finding she stood directly toward them, feared the event, and weighed their anchor, which they had but lately let go, and stood off. Captain Barnet gave them chase, and, having advantage of little breezes of wind, which blew off the land, came up with her. The captured ship was brought to Port Royal, in Jamaica and about a fortnight after the prisoners were brought ashore, viz. November 16, 1720, Captain Rackam and eight of his men were condemned and executed. Captain Rackam and two others were hung in chains.

But what was very surprising was the conviction of the nine men that came aboard the sloop on the same day she was taken. They were tried at an adjournment of the court on the January 24, the magistracy waiting all that time, it is supposed, for evidence to prove the piratical intention of going aboard the said sloop; for it seems there was no act of piracy committed by them, as appeared by the witnesses against them, two Frenchmen, taken by Rackam off the island of Hispaniola, who merely deposed that the prisoners came on board without any compulsion.

The court considered the prisoners' cases, and the majority of the commissioners being of opinion that they were all guilty of the piracy and felony they were charged with, going over with a piratical intent to John Rackam and company, then notorious pirates, and by them known to be so, they all received sentence of death, and were executed on the 17th of February at Gallows Point at Port Royal.

Rackam, as his story is related, requested a final farewell with his lover Anne Bonney, but received little comfort from her as she, expecting a child, sulked in her own jail cell.

Anne Bonney is portrayed in her tale as a pretty young woman raised with ample means, but a lack of morals. She leaves her lawful, sailor husband for a life on the lam with one of the Caribbean's last pirates, Captain Jack Rackam. Taken from *The History of Piracy*.

Anne Bonney

This female pirate was a native of Cork. Her father was an attorney, and, by his activity in business, rose to considerable respectability in that place. Anne was the fruit of an unlawful connection with his own servant maid, with whom he afterwards eloped to America, leaving his own affectionate and lawful wife. He settled at Carolina, and for some time followed his own profession; but soon commenced in the merchant trade, and was so successful as to purchase a considerable plantation. There he lived with his servant in the character of his wife; but she dying, his daughter Anne superintended the domestic affairs of her father.

During her residence with her parent she was supposed to have a considerable fortune, and was accordingly addressed by young men of respectable situations in life. It happened with Anne, however, as with many others of her youth and sex, that her feelings, and not her interest, determined her choice of a husband. She married a young sailor without a shilling. The avaricious father was so enraged that, deaf to the feelings of a parent, he turned his own child out of doors. In Philip Gosse's colorful account, the new husband, realizing his wife hadn't changed his fortunes, left town and was never seen again. In Johnson's tale, she left her husband when a better prize came along.

Anne's affections were soon stolen by pirate Captain John Rackam, nicknamed Calico Jack in the Gosse account. Eloping with him, she went to sea in men's clothes. Proving with child, the captain put her on shore, and entrusted her to the care of some friends until her recovery, when she again accompanied him in his expeditions, "as active as any with cutlass and marlinspike, always one fo the first to board a prize."

14

Anne stayed by Rackam's side through both legal and illegal endeavors. When the king offered a pardon to all pirates, Rackam surrendered, and went into the privateering business, which essentially offered pirates a legal grounds for plundering Spanish ships. However, Rackam soon veered off the allowable path, embracing an opportunity to return to his favorite employment. In all his piratical exploits Anne accompanied him; and, as we have already recorded, displayed such courage and intrepidity, that she, along with Mary Read and a seaman, were the last three who remained on board when the vessel was taken.

Anne was known to many of the planters in Jamaica, who remembered to have seen her in her father's house, and they were disposed to intercede in her behalf. Her unprincipled conduct, in leaving her own husband and forming an illicit connection with Rackam, tended, however, to render her friends less active. By a special favor, Rackam was permitted to visit her the day before he was executed; but, instead of condoling with him on account of his sad fate, she only observed, that she was sorry to see him there, but if he had fought like a man he needed not have been hanged like a dog. Being with child, she remained in prison until her recovery, was reprieved from time to time, and though we cannot communicate to our readers any particulars of her future life, or the manner of her death, yet it is certain that she was not executed.

Mary Read is portrayed as a woman who had little choice in her crossover to male imitator. A brief stint as the wife of a fellow soldier ended with his death, and Mary was forced back into her male role and military service, somehow falling into piracy. Taken from *The History of Piracy.*

Mary Read is portrayed in a wood-block print, besting an opponent. Far from flattering, the image helps to explain how she passed for a man among her shipmates.

Mary Read

Mary Read was a native of England, but at what place she was born is not recorded. Her mother married a sailor when she was very young who, soon after their marriage, went to sea, and never returned. The fruit of that marriage was a sprightly boy. The husband not returning, she again found herself with child and, to cover her shame, took leave of her husband's relations, and went to live in the country, taking her boy along with her. Her son in a short time died, and she was relieved from the burden of his maintenance and education. The mother had not resided long in the country before Mary Read, the subject of the present narrative, was born.

After the birth of Mary, her mother resided in the country for three or four years, until her money was all spent, and her ingenuity was set at work to contrive how to obtain a supply. She knew that her husband's mother was in good circumstances, and could easily support her child, provided she could make her pass for a boy, and her son's child. But it seemed impossible to impose upon an old experienced mother. She, however, presented Mary in the character of her grandson. The old woman proposed to take the boy to live with her, but the mother would not on any account part with her boy; the grandmother, therefore, allowed a crown per week for his support.

The ingenuity of the mother being successful, she reared the daughter as a boy. But as she grew up, she informed her of the secret of her birth, in order that she might conceal her sex. The grandmother, however, died and the mother was obliged to hire her daughter as a footboy to a French lady. The strength and manly disposition of this supposed boy increased with her years, and leaving that servile employment, she engaged on board a man-of-war.

The volatile disposition of the youth did not permit her to remain long in this station, and she next went into Flanders, and joined a regiment of foot as a cadet. Though in every action she conducted herself with the greatest bravery, yet she could not obtain a commission, as they were in general bought and sold. She accordingly quitted that service, and enlisted into a regiment of horse; there she behaved herself so valiantly, that she gained the esteem of all her officers. It, however, happened, that her comrade was a handsome young Fleming, and she fell passionately in love with him. The violence of her feelings rendered her negligent of her duty, and effected such a change in her behaviour as attracted the attention of all. Both her comrade and the rest of the regiment deemed her mad. Love, however, is inventive, and as they slept in the same tent, she found means to discover her sex without any seeming design. He was both surprised and pleased, supposing that he would have a mistress to himself; but he was greatly mistaken, and he found that it was necessary to court her for his wife. A mutual attachment took place, and, as soon as convenient, women's clothes were provided for her, and they were publicly married.

The singularity of two troopers marrying caused a general conversation, and many of the officers honored the ceremony with their presence, and resolved to make presents to the bride, to provide her with necessaries. After marriage they were desirous to quit the service, and their discharge being easily obtained, they set up an ordinary under the sign of the "Three Shoes," and soon acquired a considerable run of business.

But Mary Read's felicity was of short duration; the husband died, and peace being concluded, her business diminished. Under these circumstances she again resumed her man's dress, and going into Holland, enlisted into a regiment of foot quartered in one of the frontier towns. But there being no prospect of preferment in time of peace, she went on board a vessel bound for the West Indies.

During the voyage, the vessel was captured by English pirates, and as Mary was the only English person on board, they detained her, and having plundered the vessel of what they chose, allowed it to depart. Mary continued in that unlawful commerce for some time, but the royal pardon being tendered to all those in the West Indies, who should, before a specified day, surrender, the crew to which she was attached, availed themselves of this, and lived quietly on shore with the fruits of their adventures. But from the want of their usual supplies, their money became exhausted; and being informed that Captain Rogers, in the island of Providence, was fitting out some vessels for privateering, Mary, with some others, repaired to that island to serve on board his privateers. We have already heard, that scarcely had the ships sailed, when some of their crews mutinied, and ran off with the ships, to pursue their former mode of life. Among these was Mary Read.

Read had frequently declared that she detested the life of a pirate, and that she was constrained to it both on the former and present occasion. It was, however, sufficiently ascertained, that both Mary Read and Anne Bonney were among the bravest and most resolute fighters of the whole crew; that when the vessel was taken, these two heroines, along with another of the pirates, were the last three upon deck; and that Mary, having in vain endeavored to rouse the courage of the crew, who had fled below, discharged a pistol amongst them, killing one and wounding another.

Nor was Mary less modest than brave; for though she had remained many years in the character of a sailor, yet no one had discovered her sex, until she was under the necessity of doing so to Anne Bonney. The reason of this was that Anne, supposing her to be a handsome fellow, became greatly enamored of her, and discovered her sex and wishes to Mary, who was thus constrained to reveal her secret to Anne. Rackam being the paramour of Bonney, and observing her partiality towards Mary, threatened to shoot her lover. So Anne also informed the captain of the sex of her companion.

Rackam was enjoined to secrecy, and here he behaved honorably; but love again assailed the conquered Mary. It was usual with the pirates to retain all the artists who were captured in the trading-vessels; among these was a very handsome young man, of engaging manners, who vanquished the heart of Mary. In a short time her love became so violent, that she took every opportunity of enjoying his company and conversation; and, after she had gained his friendship, discovered her sex. Esteem and friendship were speedily converted into the most ardent affection, and a mutual flame burned in the hearts of these two lovers. An occurrence soon happened that put the attachment of Mary to a severe trial. Her lover having quarreled with one of the crew, they agreed to fight a duel on shore. Mary was all anxiety for the fate of her lover, and she manifested a greater concern for the preservation of his life than that of her own; but she could not entertain the idea that he could refuse to fight, and so be esteemed a coward. Accordingly she quarreled with the man who challenged her lover, and called him to the field two hours before his appointment with her lover, engaged him with sword and pistol, and laid him dead at her feet.

Though no esteem or love had formerly existed, this action was sufficient to have kindled the most violent flame. But this was not necessary, for the lover's attachment was equal, if not stronger than her own; they pledged their faith, which was esteemed as binding as if the ceremony had been performed by a clergyman.

Captain Rackam one day, before he knew that she was a woman, asked her why she followed a line of life that exposed her to so much danger, and at last to the certainty of being hanged. She replied, that, "As to hanging, she thought it no great hardship, for were it not for that, every cowardly fellow would turn pirate, and so infest the seas; and men of courage would starve. That if it was put to her choice, she would not have the punishment less than death, the fear of which kept some dastardly rogues honest; that many of those who are now cheating the widows and orphans, and oppressing their poor neighbors who have no money to obtain justice, would then rob at sea, and the ocean would be as crowded with rogues as the land: so that no merchants would venture out, and the trade in a little time would not be worth following."

Being with child at the time of her trial, her execution was delayed; and it is probable that she would have found favor, but in the mean time she fell sick and died.

"Mary Read was of a strong and robust constitution, capable of enduring much exertion and fatigue," Johnson wrote. "She was vain and bold in her disposition, but susceptible of the most tender emotions, and of the most melting affections. Her conduct was generally directed by virtuous principles, while at the same time, she was violent in her attachments. Though she was inadvertently drawn into that dishonorable mode of life which has stained her character, and given her a place among the criminals noticed in this work, yet she possessed a rectitude of principle and of conduct, far superior to many who have not been exposed to such temptations to swerve from the path of female virtue and honor."

A rendition of Alwilda from *The Pirates Own Book*.

Alwilda

Danish history contains an account of a Viking princess who turned to piracy to support a hard-won independence from her extraordinarily strict father.

Alwilda was the daughter of Gotland's king, Synardis or Siward, sometime during the 9th century AD. Her story is one of the great Gothic legends, a full-fledged fairytale with a brave and beautiful princess, a worthy prince, swashbuckling action, and a happily ever after ending.

The story is set on Gotland, Sweden's largest island, though a full 90 kilometers removed from the mainland in the Baltic Sea. Desolate mores, limestone formations, treacherous tall cliffs, and long sandy beaches characterize the island. Historically, it is a place still firmly grounded in the Middle Ages, with over 95 medieval churches dotted about the countryside as well as the ruins of many hilltop forts. The island's main city, Visby, is known for its medieval houses and alleyways, and plays host to an annual Medieval Festival that draws thousands of tourists and re-enactors to this remote place that, outwardly seems to have escaped time.

As the medieval story is related, Alwilda's father locked her in her chambers, guarded by two poisonous snakes to ward off would-be suitors. The ground rules her parents set were that any suitor brave and able enough to rescue the princess, would be granted her hand in marriage.

The task was accomplished by Prince Alf, son of Denmark's King Sygarus. Having passed the rescue test, he stilled faced parents who were reluctant to marry their daughter, and a bride who was even more reluctant. Legend relates that her own mother whispered her doubts regarding Prince

Alf's worthiness into her daughter's ear. At this point Alwilda took matters into her own hands, running away from home. The best place for a princess to disappear was most obviously the port, a place bustling with traders and seafarers congregated by the shore. She soon found herself in the company of a roving band of cross-dressing women.

Early in her voyages among the disguised women, Alwilda and her female gang set ashore in a port where a gang of pirates was mourning the recent loss of their commander. Alwilda won them over with her beauty and charms, and despite a seeming lack of seafaring experience, she was unanimously elected the new leader of the band. Together the band became a formidable force, raiding ships and settlements within the Baltic and North Seas region.

They were such a nuisance, in fact, that the Danes dispatched a military force to reign them in. And in a twist of tale ever fitting for legend, this force was led by none other than the scorned Prince Alf.

In the ensuing battles, Alwilda was said to have sustained Alf's attacks with great courage and talent, but her ship was overwhelmed in the Gulf of Finland, and Prince Alf and his crew boarded and killed the greater part of the pirate forces. Alf himself seized the captain, who was, of course, Alwilda in disguise. When he removed her helmet he discovered his unrequited love. This time, whether via the merits of his valor in combat, or the fact that he had her at his mercy, he managed to persuade the princess to marry him. The marriage took place at sea, and back home Alwilda ascended to the Danish throne as queen, eventually bearing Alf a daughter named Gurith.

Thus Alwilda's legend was assured, and her tale recorded within the *Gesta Danorum*, sixteen books of Danish history recorded by one Saxo Grammaticus, who was believed to have lived approximately 1150-1220. Her story also became legend, embellished and relished in traditional Viking sagas, intertwined with Valkyrian lore. In Scandinavian mythology, Valkyria was one of the goddess maidens both beautiful and awful, who presided over war and marked out those to be slain in battle. In fact, Alwilda is but one of many women who made her mark as a warrior in Viking history.

Her fame spread to the west in the 1800s as she entered into the annals of pirate lore, most notably in an 1837 account in *The Pirates Own Book: Authentic Narratives of the Most Celebrated Sea Robbers*, by Charles Ellms.

Charlotte de Berry

The following account is abridged from a story first published in *The History of the Pirates* in 1836 by Edward Lloyd. His "penny dreadful" account, as such popular publishing ventures were called, is without question a fabricated fiction conjured up to entertain bloodthirsty readers in Britain. Still, Charlotte de Berry's legendary figure has become one of the mainstays of female pirate lore, and there are those who cling to a kernel of truth surrounding her name and infamous career.

Though given a French name, Charlotte de Berry was born in England in the year 1636. Her parents were poor but respectable people. Her father had formerly been a ship-owner to some considerable extents, but having met with innumerable disasters and misfortunes at sea, he was compelled at last to retire from that hazardous profession and, at the urgent solicitations of his wife, retired upon the wreck of his fortune. He devoted himself instead to the care and instruction of his only child, the heroine of the following narrative.

Charlotte was a very pretty and sensible child, and her father, being a most accomplished man, took a pride in cultivating her mind. By the age of fourteen she was considered not only one of the most handsome, but intellectual young ladies in their region. She was very tall, with a most graceful person, a noble countenance, dark penetrating eye, a cheek always rosy with health, and dimpled with the smile of good humor. Yet she was also spirited, passionate, tyrannical, and unforgiving, offering early proofs for the recklessness and determined temper that afterwards so singularly distinguished her.

It happened that when our heroine was born, and the place where she passed all her youthful days, was a seaport town and in consequence of that, it was almost always full of sailors. Strange as it may appear, Charlotte, from a child, expressed her regret that she was not a man, and evinced all the hardihood, spirit, and energy of the opposite sex. She worshipped the sea almost as much as the Deity, and felt a most singular and striking regard for a sailor. She would wander daily to the beach, and watch vessels sail into port, with a feeling of the most unbounded delight. Unbeknownst to her parents, she was known to dress in male attire and visit public houses frequented by the sailors. On such an occasion she met with one Jack Jib, a rough-spun, jolly, good hearted, and weather-beaten career seaman in the British Navy. He won her heart, and her hand. Charlotte eloped with him, and when he was ordered to sea, she enlisted as his "brother" in order to follow him. Aboard this ship, Charlotte fought in no less than six military engagements, and received the highest encomiums from her officers, and the promise of promotion.

Charlotte bore an ardent affection for her plain and honest husband, and he felt a sincere regard for his wife. She always fought by his side, shared in every danger, and had been the means of rescuing him from the sword of the enemy no less than four times. Their extreme friendship for each other often surprised the men in the ship, but still they had no suspicion of Charlotte's real sex. After being engaged in several enterprises with her husband, a circumstance occurred, which turned the current of her feelings in a moment, and filled her mind with enmity to mankind; and the Navy especially, which subsided only with her death, and which afterwards made her so terrible to all who heard even her name mentioned.

In some accounts, Jack Jib, by some means or other, offended the lieutenant, who was a cruel and upstart tyrant. In others, the lieutenant learns of Charlotte's true identity, and determined to have her for himself, tries to strike a deal with the couple. Unsuccessful in this attempt, the villain accused Jack Jib of attempted mutiny, for which he was brought to court martial and sentenced to be flogged through the fleet, meaning whipped on every boat in the harbor. This inhuman sentence was carried into effect; and poor Jack Jib endured his punishment with great fortitude, never uttering a groan. However, the flogging took its intended toll, and he died a week later.

The fleet soon afterward arrived at home, and Charlotte, arming herself with a couple of pistols, laid wait for the lieutenant at night, in a lane through which she knew he had to pass. It was not long before he arrived at the spot where she was waiting, and the next minute he was but a corpse on the earth. She then stripped him of all the property he had about him, which was a considerable sum in money.

Charlotte's parents were said to have died of a broken heart when their daughter eloped to sea. So there was no going home. She made her way to London, where she resumed her female habiliments. In some accounts, Charlotte used her new wealth to earn a place in high society, where she was admired by society's upper echelon and welcomed to their affairs and functions. In others, she worked as an entertainer in the same saloons she used to frequent for fun.

In either case, Charlotte soon attracted the attentions of a merchant vessel captain, Captain Wilmington, who took such a fancy to her that he vowed a most fervent affection for her and made her an offer of marriage. Charlotte, however, advised him that she would never be his, and cryptically warned him against the danger in forming a passion for one whom he might have reason to curse. Still, the captain persisted in his vows, and finding that she was not to be won by a promise of marriage, he made several attempts to seduce her. Undaunted, he finally succeeded in waylaying her, bore her on board his vessel, and immediately set sail for the coast of Guinea. Forced to submit to his embraces, Charlotte harboured an implacable hatred towards him, and vowed never to rest till she had been avenged for the triumph he had gained over her. With this goal in mind, she watched for her opportunity in secret, and so well disguised her real sentiments, that the captain had no suspicion of her cruel designs.

Captain Wilmington was a very severe man, and was continually punishing the seamen for the most trivial offences; in consequence of which most of them heartily hated him, and only wanted a determined leader, to make them break forth into open mutiny. They found that determined leader where they had least expected it, in the person of Charlotte de Berry. She was a great favourite with the crew, who admired her pretty features, her general affable temper, and freedom of manners, and sincerely pitied her for the dupe she had been made by the treachery of their captain. In several instances Charlotte had saved more than one of them from punishment, and their hearts in consequence were overflowing with gratitude towards her. Charlotte was aware of the influence she possessed over the men, and she had likewise watched their sullen look towards the captain, and overheard their murmurs of dissatisfaction. She was resolved to await a fitting opportunity in which to make herself mistress of the ship.

When they had been out at sea about a month, they found it necessary to put in at a small island for fresh water. Many of the seamen went on shore, and Charlotte got the captain's permission to do the same, for the purpose (as aforesaid,) of seeing the island. The men, some seven in number, were some distance in advance of her, and did not notice Charlotte following them. She suspected that they were about to form some stratagem to be avenged on the captain, and that would consequently be a good time for her to put her own plans into execution. The sailors having arrived at a deep cluster of trees, formed themselves into a group, and commenced a secret consultation. Charlotte eavesdropped as they expressed their dissatisfaction with the captain and their wish to murder him, seize the vessel, and become pirates. But not one of them was bold enough to offer himself as the leader of their secret conspiracy. When Charlotte presented herself to the conspiring crew, the men leapt up in fear. One of them cried out "We are betrayed!" and drew his cutlass to strike Charlotte. She exclaimed, "Hold! I am your friend; alike the enemy of Captain Wilmington, and burning for revenge. I have overheard all you have said. Only swear to be faithful to me, and I will rid you of your cares, and place the vessel in your hands this very night."

The sailors could scarcely credit their ears; but when they had somewhat recovered from the astonishment into which it had thrown them, they expressed their admiration of the heroism of Charlotte, by loud shouts of applause, and agreed to be guided by her in everything. She then revealed to them her former history, the service she had seen, and her resolution to again assume the male attire, and to turn pirate. The sailors very highly applauded this singular determination, and promised to obey her mandates as faithfully as if she was one of their own sex, and to stand firm by her in whatever peril they might encounter. They then began to plan the assassination of the captain; whom Charlotte proposed murdering with her own hands, when they had retired for the night to their cabin. After she had accomplished this deed, she would signal her fellow mutineers by blowing a particular signal on the boatswain's whistle, at which point they were to rush forth, seize all who offered any resistance, and, at all hazards, make the vessel their own. Charlotte then returned first to the ship, while the sailors procured fresh water and other necessaries. All back on board, the ill-fated Captain Wilmington was not the least suspicious.

Upon the hour for retiring to rest, the captain appeared more than usually affectionate, but his kindness only served to inflame the hot blood of the desperate woman the more, and she waited impatiently for sleep to render him insensible to her actions. When that fatal moment at last arrived, Charlotte arose cautiously, got a sharp knife, which she had concealed in the cabin, and at one stroke nearly severed her victim's head from his body. She then gave the signal agreed upon, and the mutineers rushed in to her assistance. They found little opposition to their will, and that only from the mate and another seaman, whom the mutineers quickly settled by tossing them overboard, and in an hour, the mutineers were complete masters of the vessel. They then shouted, "Long life and success to the gallant female pirate captain, Charlotte de Berry!"

Thus began Charlotte's criminal career as a pirate. She immediately assumed male attire, and never divested herself of them again on the ocean. She went by the name of Captain Rodolph, and she named her ship The Trader. She soon spread a great panic among trading vessels, particularly on the African coast, where she prowled in quest of the ships which traded for gold dust. Her engagements were generally very decisive; for nothing could daunt the courage of her invincible crew; and when they were triumphant, they dealt most unmercifully with those prisoners who refused to join them, putting them to cruel deaths, and plundering them of all they possessed. Rumors spread about her ferocity and cruelty. One claimed she had sewn shut one captain's mouth

It happened once, that as her crew was cruising about their usual hunting grounds along the coast of Africa, they spied a ship of moderate size making full sail towards them. From the colors which were flying at the mast head, that she was an English vessel; and, as it approached nearer, she found it was a brig carrying several guns, and seemingly well prepared to meet any private ships that might cross her path. Nevertheless, Charlotte, with her usual courage and daring, resolved to attack her, and accordingly put her vessel into proper order, for the bloody action that was soon fated to take place. Suspecting by the size of the enemy and the manner in which the brig was armed, that she had a valuable cargo aboard, Charlotte was determined to become the mistress or perish in the attempt. The ship soon came within gun-shot of them, and proved to be the an English ship, homeward bound, carrying eighteen guns, together with a valuable cargo of gold-dust, and having on board twenty one seamen and twelve passengers

This was a very formidable foe, but Charlotte was not at all daunted, and quickly hoisting the black flag, called upon the enemy to strike! A loud laugh from the British crew was the answer to this order, and our heroine, enraged at this, gave orders for a heavy broadside upon the English ship, which carried away one of the masts, and killed the lieutenant and two of the female passengers. The battle that now ensued baffles all description; both parties fought desperately, but yet with unparalleled judgment and coolness.

Never had Charlotte met with a more equal match, and never did she purchase a dearer conquest. Three times did the pirates board the brig, and again were driven back with great slaughter. Both vessels were nearly battered to pieces, and numbers were slain. The pirate crew was reduced to eight, and the British brig had lost its captain, lieutenant, and several of the crew, in spite of which the sailors continued the struggle with unabated courage, and seemed resolved never to yield to the pirates while they had a man left. In this critical state of affairs, when Charlotte beheld her men fast falling around her, and nothing but ruin seemed to stare her in the face, she resolved to make a final and desperate effort, even if it cost her her life.

The enemy were making an attempt to board them, and the pirates being somewhat daunted by the manly courage of their foes, and the number of their comrades that had fallen around them, seemed half inclined to yield, when Charlotte rushed forward with a pistol in each hand, and aroused them to once more act like men. They went boldly to the attack; their heroic female captain bravely leading the way, and being resolved to repel the foes who were now fast rushing on board the pirate ship and committing great havoc around them. In an instant a couple of the pirates who were by the side of our heroine, were stretched dead at her feet; but at the same moment, she fired and shot the leader of the Englishmen, who fell backwards into the raging deep, and her other pistol felled his companion in the like manner.

The rest of the enemy, daunted by Charlotte's courage, were completely defeated and endeavored to regain their vessel in the utmost terror and confusion. Many of them fell into the ocean, and those who did get back to the ship quickly met their fate, for the brig had been so dreadfully knocked about in the strife that she quickly filled, and sunk like a shot, with all her treasure onboard! Thus Charlotte lost a very rich prize, and at great cost. It was with extreme difficulty that she managed to get her own vessel into a little creek close by, with the remnant of her daring crew. Here she had the ship repaired, and in a few days put to sea again, though she had now but a small number of men, and did not intend to venture any other attack until she had got more hands on board, and the survivors had recovered from the recent panic into which the battle had thrown them.

Charlotte de Berry, when ashore, always resumed her female apparel, and passed off as a passenger onboard the Trader. Her lieutenant, an intelligent man, always attended her, posing as her uncle and a rich merchant. As such, they were invited into the best society. Charlotte was still a beautiful woman, and excited universal admiration wherever she appeared.

It happened that, having put into Grenada, our heroine as usual doffed her male attire, and appeared in her own character; and there she attracted the attention of a wealthy planter's son. This young man, who was not more than twenty two years of age, was so struck with her charms that he made an immediate-disclosure of his sentiments and implored her to look with favor upon his suit. Charlotte was pleased with the young man's candour, and the gracefulness of his person, and felt for him an affection as ardent as that she had felt for her husband. She therefore received his suit with favor, and consented to a clandestine marriage. Their passions confessed and the nuptials accomplished, Charlotte made him acquainted with her real character, and left it to his own discretion and free will to follow the same lawless course with her, or abandon her forever. Such was the strength of the youth's attachment to this extraordinary woman, that he directly came to the former resolution, swore fidelity to his wife, and ran away with her on board the pirate ship after inducing many of his father's slaves to accompany him. Thus the vessel was speedily well manned again and she set sail in company with her new made husband, upon fresh adventures. He proved, in a very short time, a most determined fellow, and fought by her side in the most resolute and heroic manner.

They had only been married three years when their pirate ship suffered severely from a tempest, was driven from their latitude, and reduced to famine and extreme distress. Such were the horrors of their situation, that for three days they tasted not a morsel of food, nor drink to slack their burning thirst, and in their horrible situation, and reduced to the most wretched condition, they at last came to the dreadful resolution they should cast lots to see which of them should die to feed their unfortunate comrades. Lots were drawn and the sacrifice fell upon the husband of our heroine! So great was her affection for him, she offered her own body to the crew. But before the crew could elect either of them, one of the black slaves, who had accompanied Charlotte's husband on his elopement from home insisted on the sacrifice of his own life, and before anyone could stop him, plunged a knife into his own heart. His body was instantly cut up, and greedily devoured by the unfortunate crew. Thus was Charlotte's husband preserved for the first time, from a horrid fate.

The slave's body lasted them only two days, and then they were in the same dreadful state of suffering as formerly, without any prospect of relief. The horrid casting of lots, for the sacrifice of one of their comrades, was again proposed, and agreed to when, by a strange fatality, the lot fell again upon Charlotte's husband. Charlotte once more offered herself instead of her husband, but was obstinately refused by the crew. Once again, our heroine's husband was preserved by the magnanimity of a negro, who slew himself in the same manner.

The second body consumed, there was as yet no help on the horizon. For the third time lots were drawn, and, as though an infernal spell rested on him, again the lot fell upon the husband of the female pirate! Being now entirely hopeless, he prepared to meet his dreadful fate, but Charlotte implored them to let him live, if it was only for two hours, to see if any succor arrived. They all consented, and sat watching, with greedy eyes, their unfortunate victim during the two hours. But no succor came. Again their female captain interfered in behalf of her husband, and begged of them to allow him but another two hours reprieve; but their famine was now raised to such an intolerable pitch, that they, one and all, declared they could hold out no longer, and advanced to seize, him. Charlotte, with tears in her eyes, begged them to desist, but they were deaf to her cries.

She next implored them to be satisfied with the calves of his legs for the present, and then, if they did not meet any help by the evening, she promised them that she would no longer oppose their will. To this they agreed, and the miserable man actually submitted, and that with great fortitude, to the dreadful torture of having his calves cut off, which the half starved wretches greedily devoured. Night soon arrived, and yet they were in the same horrible situation; the pirates now declared that if their victim was not given up to them, they would have both Charlotte and him likewise. Finding, it useless to resist, she took an affectionate leave of her unfortunate husband, who begged to be shot, and that they would not feast upon him until they were convinced that his life was quite extinct. To this the pirates promised obedience.

No sooner had he fallen, than the pirates stripped off his clothes and commenced cutting up the body, and devouring it while yet the vital warmth remained in it. One of the monsters had even the cruelty to offer Charlotte a portion of the dreadful meat, but she turned from him with disgust, and hastened down below to give vent to her grief. She had not long been there, when she heard a great confusion upon deck, and cries of "A sail! A sail!" In an instant she rushed upon deck, as well as her strength would permit her, and there indeed beheld a vessel making full sail toward them, which proved to be an English ship.

On seeing their signals of distress, the British vessel immediately manned a couple of boats and sent them, with all possible dispatch, to the pirate ship. The pirates related a false tale about their being French sailors, attacked by pirates. According to their story, the pirates had stripped their vessel of everything valuable, threw their provisions overboard, and murdered the greater portion of their crew, then left them to their fates. The boats instantly returned to their ship, and the English captain, being a very kind-hearted, honest Englishman, did not doubt, for a moment, the truth of their story, and was very much affected at the sufferings of the crew. He therefore sent them enough provisions and grog to last them till they reached a port, from which, he said, they were no considerable distance. The men aboard the pirate ship now made a hearty meal, but Charlotte was too much affected at the horrible fate of her husband to eat much.

Charlotte was so shocked by the death of her husband that she became a complete idiot, and the command of the vessel was therefore committed to the lieutenant. Though several of the ruffians proposed throwing her overboard; the majority of her shipmates insisted that she be suffered to wander about the ship muttering her wild ravings. Soon after this, the pirates attacked a Dutch trading ship of large size and force, upon which the maniac Charlotte insisted upon being attired in her usual apparel, and with a pistol in each hand, performed wonders, slaying all who ventured near her. At length, she received a blow from a cutlass, and fell overboard, exclaiming "My husband! Thy bride, Charlotte, the female pirate, comes to join thee!" The pirates fought as long as they were able, and then blew the vessel into the air; thus escaping that punishment allotted to them, if they had been taken.

As pirate aficionados argue, Charlotte walked a thin plank dividing society's good from evil. After all, she first served within the Navy, which was actively jostling for imperial control of territories in Asia, Africa, and the "New World," with little regard for the well being of the original inhabitants, and with every intent of bringing the riches of these far off lands home. Next she sailed, albeit unwillingly, aboard a trading ship that was probably actively engaged in Europe's legal, though, brutal, imperialism. Kidnapped and raped by a legal captain, she crossed into the realm of outlaw only after killing her captor and preying upon ships laden with gold and slaves stolen out of Africa. Charlotte lived and prospered in a very brutal era, and proved a formidable competitor within a realm reserved primarily for men.

Grace O'Malley

While the word "pirate" is generally equivalent with "criminal," and often worse, there have been periods in history where their offensive acts on the high seas were considered great acts of patriotism. Among the Irish, where a long struggle for independence from England is part and parcel of the national character, it is hard to imagine a greater sense of pride than that harbored for the homegrown pirate queen Grace O'Malley. She grew so powerful that she was able to command an audience with Queen Elizabeth I, and she commanded a small army of men willing to sacrifice their lives for her.

Born to a long line of seafarers dating back to 1123, some even say that Grace O'Malley, or Gráinne Ni Mháille as she was properly named, was born aboard a ship. She came into the world circa 1530, and soon distinguished herself as a girl who wouldn't be content to care for the household. Her father was Owen O'Maley, the elected chieftain of the Barony of Murrisk, a coastal territory that included the south shore of Clew Bay and Clare Island, where Grace was reportedly born. Owen also acted as sea captain and regularly staged trading voyages to Spain and Scotland. Grace's mother, Margaret O'Malley, was a noblewoman from another branch of the clan.

Growing up on the Island of Clare, Grace was said to be quite the tomboy, attempting early on to impress her father that she was as capable as any boy to work aboard his ships. Cutting off her long hair and donning boy's cloths to prove her point earned her the nickname, Gráinne Mhoal or Bald Grace, a pseudonym often used in the legends and stories that surround her life by the Irish who grew so fond of her. Those who feared her - chief among them British traders and landlords - came to call her The Irish Sea Queen and The Pirate Queen of Connaught.

Eventually her father relented and let her onboard his small fleet of ships, and it became clear that she would make her life as a seafarer. She proved her prowess first on the other side of a pirate's cutlass.

Grace and her father were sailing during treacherous times upon the sea. British "privateers" prowled the waters with immunity, operating with the blessings of the Queen, and sometimes government support in a mandate to interrupt and impoverish Spanish trade ships. This because the Spanish worked against other European powers in restricting trade with their massive and wealthy colonies in the New World. So any ship suspected of hauling Spanish dubloons was considered a free-for-all on the seas, and equally at risk were those who traded with Spain, in this case the O'Malley clan.

Worse, the Irish were being subjected to a British policy of "Submit and Regrant" established by Henry VIII. Under these terms, Irish chieftains were allowed to keep their land only if they accepted English rule, and abided by restrictions against the transport of goods by any ships other than British.

So Grace and her father knew trouble was afoot when they spied a British ship sailing their way. Her father ordered her below for safety. However, Grace was never one to cower - instead she climbed into the rigging. From her perch she watched the battle that ensued and, witnessing a pirate sneak up behind her father, she fell upon him kicking, screaming, and biting. Having saved her father, she had only just began to earn her fearsome reputation.

She married at the age of 16 and went to live with her new

44

family in Connacht. Yet, though she bore three children - Owen, Murrough, and Margaret - Grace didn't disappear into domestic duties. Grace had wed Donal O'Flaherty, an heir in the complicated and contentious succession to chief position among the O'Flaherty clan. He was said to be a fearsome fighter, but with a terrible temper and an irresponsible streak that nearly bankrupted the clan. Grace helped to build the family's sea trading business, and was soon running most of their affairs. Grace was by her husband's side during a battle with a rival clan, the Joyces, in 1565. When Donal was killed, Grace fought on and helped to defeat her husband's killers. However, the deed earned her little credit with his family, as she was given no portion of the estate and returned penniless with her children to O'Malley territory. There she embarked on a career that earned her a preeminent place in the pirate hall of fame.

Recruiting a crew of 200 men, Grace began to patrol the coast around her home base of Clare Island, demanding protection money from passing ships or forcing them to hire her navigators. Sometimes she simply turned her pirates loose to plunder what they would. She was not above murder, either, and was said to have personally administered death to men who murdered her lover.

Within a year, she was married again, a strategic marriage that gave her control of Rockfleet Castle and all of Clew Bay. Apparently there was love between herself and Richard Burke, as the two had a son, Tibbott-ne-Long (Toby of the Ships). Once again, it is said that Grace quickly gained control in the marriage, and took control of the castle and the surrounding territory. In one version of the story, Grace took advantage of a widely practice loophole in the traditional Brehon legal system, divorcing her husband within a year of their nuptials, but not before she gained control of the castle and the surrounding territory. In another version, she threatens divorce but never carries through. In all the stories, the two stay together for seventeen years, until Richard dies.

Legends holds that their son was born aboard ship. At 37 years old, Grace must have been exhausted by her labors, yet she came upon deck the very next day to fight off an attack by Turkish pirates.

Grace's fleet numbered some twenty ships by the early 1570s, and her piratical presence was becoming an increasingly felt menace among the English merchants who plied the Irish coast. In response to the pleas of merchants, the crown sent vessels to lay siege to Grace's Rockfleet Castle in 1574, but she mustered her own forces and sent them packing.

Three years later, Grace was captured as she led a raid on the Earl of Desmond's lands, and spent the next eighteen months a prisoner in a Limerick jail. Here Lord Justice Drury labeled her in terms that have left generations of Irish Nationalists seething. Drury described her as "a woman that hath impudently passed the part of womanhood and been a great spoiler and chief commander and director of thieves and murderers at sea." This seemed to spell the end of Grace's career and life, but somehow she negotiated her release from the prison - no doubt cashing in on the same nationalist appeal that has earned her centuries of ensuing fame on the Emerald Isle. She was soon back at work, disrupting English commerce and conducting land raids at the head of her private army.

Sir Richard Bingham came close to stopping her in 1586. Appointed Governor of the region, he was wildly unpopular. He was evicting the Irish chieftains and nobles and redistributing their lands as he saw fit, and as if this weren't enough, he seemed bent upon eradicating Gaelic culture and replace

46

local customs with English norms. Grace was a heroine among the many rebels resisting him, and he dealt with her by murdering her own son, Owen O'Flaherty, capturing Grace and her small army, and seizing all of their property. Sir Richard ordered that a gallows be constructed to deal justice to the pirates, and Grace was reportedly brave in facing her death. However, she was spared by the sacrifice of her son-in-law, who took her place as captive.

Impoverished again, Grace resumed her life as raider and pirate, and Sir Richard continued to oppress the natives of his region. The Irish were in continual revolt against Sir Richard, and Grace's efforts were undoubtedly applied with the goal of unseating him. In fact, she began a letter-writing campaign to Queen Elizabeth I, complaining of Sir Richard's unjust treatment of his constituency. Surprisingly, the queen responded with a letter containing Eighteen Articles of Interogatory, and in response Sir Richard clapped Grace's sons, Murrough and Tibbott, and her brother Donell O'Piper in irons. This was the last straw for Grace. She set sail for England, to seek audience with the queen.

When she arrived at the court of Queen Elizabeth in September 1593, Grace was permitted an audience with the queen. Defiantly presenting herself, a bold and swarthy woman in her sixties, before a court of powdered and primped men and women, O'Malley had quite an impact. Legend has it that the two women became friends. Fact has it that Grace left England with a pardon from the queen, and orders that Sir Richard release Grace's sons and brother, and provide a living for the family of his steadfast enemy. Within two years, the Queen had appointed a replacement for Sir Richard.

Grace never gave up her pirating ways. She continued to command a fleet of ships until her death at a ripe old age. Some legends hold that Grace O'Malley died during a raid on a merchant ship; others that advancing age kept her ashore, commanding her ships from the stronghold of her castle Rockfleet. She died in 1603, approximately 75 years old and a pirate until the end.

Madame Ching is portrayed in action in a woodblock print.

Madam Ching

For three years, a Chinese woman rose to lead one of the largest pirate fleets the world has ever known. At the height of her power, in 1809, her pirate confederation outmanned, out-gunned, and outnumbered the fleets claimed by most of the world's navies. These pirates swarmed the seas around Southern China, raiding merchant and fishing vessels, and running a protection racket that kept even inland villages in tribute to the forces commanded by Ching.

The Ladrones, as they were christened by the Portuguese at Macao, were originally a disaffected set of Chinese that revolted against the oppression of the Mandarins. The first scene of their depredations was the Western coast, about Cochin China, where they began by attacking small trading vessels in rowboats, carrying from thirty to forty men each. They continued this system of piracy, and thrived and increased in numbers under it, for several years. At length the fame of their success lured many impoverished Chinese, who labored in horrid poverty and oppression under Mandarin rule. Fishermen and other destitute classes flocked by the hundreds to the pirate's standard, and their audacity grew with their numbers.

They not only swept the coast, but blockaded all the rivers and attacked and took several large government war junks, mounting from ten to fifteen guns each. Thus the Chinese pirates formed a tremendous fleet, which was always along shore, so that no small vessel could safely trade on the coast. When they lacked prey on the sea, they laid the land under tribute. They were at first accustomed to go on shore and attack the maritime villages, but becoming bolder they made long inland journeys, and surprised and plundered even large towns.

Ching Yi Sao, or Ching Shih, entered the picture in 1901 when she married Ching Yi, leader of the pirate confederation. A former prostitute from Canton, little is known about her personal life or physical appearance. However, the exploits of the "Ladrone" and attempts to rid the coast of them, are well documented in China.

Ching Yi, through valor and conduct, obtained by degrees a supremacy of command over the whole united fleet. His power and means multiplied daily with the force of his vast fleet, and he aspired to the dignity of a king. He went so far as to openly declare his patriotic intention of hurling the present Tartar family from the throne of China, and of restoring the ancient Chinese dynasty. But unfortunately for the ambitious pirate, he perished in a heavy gale, and instead of placing a sovereign on the Chinese throne, he and his lofty aspirations were buried in the yellow sea in 1807.

Ching Yi Sao, which means "wife of Ching," assumed power after her husband's death. Such a move was not considered out of line in a culture where women often rose to power through marriage. Nor were women unusual in the floating world off the China coast. Entire families lived in the cramped environments of small fishing boats and the larger junks, many with no piece of land to call home, and a rare need to step ashore. Just as the women assisted their husbands in fishing duties, so they lent a hand when the family changed trades to privateering.

The Ladrones had no settled residence on shore, but lived constantly in their vessels. On the larger junks, the after part was occupied by the captain and his wives - generally he kept five or six. With respect to the conjugal rights, the Ladrones were religiously strict. No person was allowed to have a woman on board unless married to her according to their laws. Every man was allowed a small berth, about four feet square, where he stowed with his wife and family.

One of Madame Ching's first acts was to appoint one Paou as her lietenant and prime minister, reserving the role of commander-in-chief of the united pirate squadrons for herself. This Paou had been a poor fisher-boy, picked up with his father at sea by Ching Yi. Through good will, favor, and skill, he had proven himself a brilliant pirate leader and was adopted by Ching I as his son. Further, within weeks of the demise of her husband, Madame Ching made Paou her lover and together they set out to rule. Instead of declining under the rule of a woman, the pirates became more enterprising than ever. Ching's widow was clever as well as brave, and so was her lieutenant, Paou. Between them they drew up a code of law to better regulate the freebooters. The newly decreed rules included:

* If any man went privately on shore he should have his ears slit in the presence of the whole fleet. A repetition of the same unlawful act was death!

* No one article, however trifling in value, was to be privately subtracted from the booty, or plundered goods.

* On a piratical expedition, either to advance or retreat without orders, was a capital offense.

* No person shall debauch at his pleasure captive women, taken in the villages and open places, and brought on board a ship; he must first request the ship's purser for permission, and then go aside in the ship's hold. To use violence against any woman, or to wed her, without permission, would be punished with death.

Rules were even set down to gentrify the pursuit of pillaging. Madame Ching forbade use of the word "plunder," instead instituting a more politically appealing "Transhipped Goods" in the pirates' terminology. A stickler for detail and a keen businesswoman, she insisted that all "Transhipped Goods" be brought to a central "warehouse" and meticulously noted in a register.

By these means discipline was maintained onboard the ships. Through plundering at sea and pillaging ashore, the pirates were never in want for gunpowder, provisions, or any other necessity. Under these philosophical institutions, and the guidance of a woman, the robbers continued to scour the China sea, plundering every vessel they came near.

For three years Madame Ching and Paou fought off forces mustered by the government to squash the pirate fleets. In 1809, one estimate held that the pirate forces consisted of 70,000 men navigating eight hundred large vessels and one thousand small ones, including rowboats, which were used to navigate shallow rivers to extract tribute from inland towns and villages. The forces were divided into six large squadrons, under different flags - the red, the yellow, the green, the blue, the black, and the white, and the swarms they formed earned them the moniker of "wasps of the Ocean." The commanders names and reputations were attached to the flags, the more notable noms de guerre being "Bird and Stone," "Scourge of the Eastern Sea," "Jewel of the Whole Crew," and "Frog's Meal."

Madame Ching proved herself as a leader, capturing the hearts and loyalties of her vast army, and as a tactician in battle. In an early example of her strategic gifts, she won victory against the imperial army in 1808. "When the Imperial vessels approached she sent against them only a few of her own, hiding the rest behind a headland. When her decoys had joined battle, she brought out her main squadrons and attacked the enemy suddenly in the rear. The fight continued from early morning until late evening, eventually defeating the Imperial fleet and causing the Admiral to take his own life in disgrace," according to Philip Gosse.

In fact, every government ship sent to thwart the pirates was defeated, and by 1908 the government had lost more than sixty war ships. Many of these were captured by Madame Ching's forces, and their war provisions were added to the might of the pirates. After the well recorded battles waged by several Chinese generals against the pirates failed, the Chinese Government resolved to cut off all the pirates' supplies of food, and starve them out. All vessels that were in port were ordered to remain there, and those at sea, or on the coast ordered to return with all speed. But the pirates, full of confidence, now resolved to attack the harbors themselves, and to ascend the rivers, which are navigable for many miles up the country, and rob the villages. The consternation was great when the Chinese saw them venturing above the government forts.

The pirates separated: Mistress Ching plundering in one place, Paou in another, O-po-tae in another, and so on.

An Englishman's Report on the Ladrones

In 1809, an Englishman, Mr. Glasspoole, had the ill fortune to fall into their power while an officer in the East India Company's ship the Marquis of Ely. He survived eleven weeks in captivity, kept alive while the pirates sent out demands for enormous ransom sums for his release.

He shared many details of his time in the company of the Ladrones, related at length in the Pirate's Own Book, including his observations of their lives at sea:

"From the number of souls crowded in so small a space, it must naturally be supposed they are horridly dirty, which is

A Ladrone fighter is portrayed collecting heads for a pirate's bounty during a pirate raid ashore.

evidently the case, and their vessels swarm with all kinds of vermin. Rats in particular, which they encourage to breed, and eat as great delicacies; in fact, there are very few creatures they will not eat. During our captivity we lived three weeks on caterpillars boiled with rice. They are much addicted to gambling, and spend all their leisure hours at cards and smoking opium."

Glasspoole's narrative illustrates the brutality with which Madam Ching's forces acted:

"Wednesday the 26th of September, at daylight, we passed in sight of our own ships at anchor under the island of Chun Po. The chief then called me, pointed to the ships, and told the interpreter to tell us to look at them, for we should never see them again! About noon we entered a river to the westward of the Bogue. Three or four miles from the entrance we passed a large town situated on the side of a beautiful hill, which is tributary to the Ladrones; the inhabitants saluted them with songs as they passed."

After committing numerous minor robberies, "The Ladrones now prepared to attack a town with a formidable force, collected in rowboats from the different vessels. They sent a messenger to the town, demanding a tribute of ten thousand dollars annually, saying, if these terms were not complied with, they would land, destroy the town, and murder all the inhabitants: which they would certainly have done, had the town laid in a more advantageous situation for their purpose; but being placed out of the reach of their shot, they allowed them to come to terms. The inhabitants agreed to pay six thousand dollars, which they were to collect by the time of our return down the river. This finesse had the desired effect, for during our absence they mounted a few guns on a hill, which commanded the passage, and gave us in lieu of the dollars, a warm salute on our return.

"October the 1st, the fleet weighed in the night, dropped by the tide up the river, and anchored very quietly before a town surrounded by a thick wood. Early in the morning the Ladrones assembled in rowboats, and landed; then gave a shout, and rushed into the town, sword in hand. The inhabitants fled to the adjacent hills, in numbers apparently superior to the Ladrones. We may easily imagine to ourselves the horror with which these miserable people must be seized, on being obliged to leave their homes, and everything dear to them. It was a most melancholy sight to see women in tears, clasping their infants in their arms, and imploring mercy for them from those brutal robbers! The old and the sick, who were unable to fly, or make resistance, were either made prisoners or most inhumanly butchered! The boats continued passing and re-passing from the junks to the shore, in quick succession, laden with booty, and the men besmeared with blood! Two hundred and fifty women and several children were made prisoners, and sent on board different vessels. They were unable to escape with the men, owing to that abominable practice of cramping their feet; several of them were not able to move without assistance. In fact, they might all be said to totter, rather than walk. Twenty of these poor women were sent on board the vessel I was in; they were hauled on board by the hair, and treated in a most savage manner. When the chief came on board, he questioned them respecting the circumstances of their friends, and demanded ransoms accordingly, from six thousand to six hundred dollars each. He ordered them a berth on deck, at the after part of the vessel where they had nothing to shelter them from the weather, which at this time was very variable - the days excessively hot, and the nights cold, with heavy rains. The town being plundered of everything valuable, it was set on fire, and reduced to ashes by the morning. The fleet remained here three days, negotiating for the ransom of the prisoners, and plundering the fish-tanks and gardens. During all this time, the Chinese never ventured from the hills, though there were frequently not more than a hundred Ladrones on shore at a time, and I am sure the people on the hills exceeded ten times that number.

"On the 10th we formed a junction with the Black-squadron, and proceeded many miles up a wide and beautiful river, passing several ruins of villages that had been destroyed by the Black-squadron. On the 17th, the fleet anchored abreast four mud batteries, which defended a town, so entirely surrounded with wood that it was impossible to form any idea of its size. The weather was very hazy, with hard squalls of rain. The Ladrones remained perfectly quiet for two days. On the third day the forts commenced a brisk fire for several hours: the Ladrones did not return a single shot, but weighed in the night and dropped down the river. The reason they gave for not attacking the town, or returning the fire, was that Joss had not promised them success. They are very superstitious, and consult their idol on all occasions. If his omens are good, they will undertake the most daring enterprises. The fleet now anchored opposite the ruins of the town where the women had been made prisoners. Here we remained five or six days, during which time about a hundred of the women were ransomed; the remainder were offered for sale amongst the Ladrones, for forty dollars each. The woman is considered the lawful wife of the purchaser, who would be put to death if he discarded her. Several of them leaped overboard and drowned themselves, rather than submit to such infamous degradation.

"Mei-ying, the wife of Ke-choo-yang, was very beautiful, and a pirate being about to seize her by the head, she abused him exceedingly. The pirate bound her to the yardarm; but on abusing him yet more, the pirate dragged her down and broke two of her teeth, which filled her mouth and jaws with blood. The pirate sprang up again to bind her. Ying allowed him to approach, but as soon as he came near her, she laid hold of his garments with her bleeding mouth, and threw both him and herself into the river, where they were drowned. The remaining captives of both sexes were after some months liberated, on having paid a ransom.

"The fleet then weighed," continues Mr. Glasspoole, "and made sail down the river, to receive the ransom from the town before-mentioned. As we passed the hill, they fired several shots at us, but without effect. The Ladrones were much exasperated, and determined to revenge themselves; they dropped out of reach of their shot, and anchored. Every junk sent about a hundred men each on shore, to cut paddy (rice), and destroy their orange-groves, which was most effectually performed for several miles down the river. During our stay here, they received information of nine boats lying up a creek, laden with paddy; boats were immediately despatched after them. Next morning these boats were brought to the fleet; ten or twelve men were taken in them. As these had made no resistance, the chief said he would allow them to become Ladrones, if they agreed to take the usual oaths before Joss. Three or four of them refused to comply, for which they were punished in the following cruel manner: their hands were tied behind their backs, a rope from the masthead rove through their arms, and hoisted three or four feet from the deck, and five or six men flogged them with their rattans twisted together till they were apparently dead; then hoisted them up to the mast-head, and left them hanging nearly an hour, then lowered them down, and repeated the punishment, till they died or complied with the oath...

"On the first of November, the fleet sailed up a narrow river, and anchored at night within two miles of a town called Little Whampoa. In front of it was a small fort, and several Mandarin vessels lying in the harbor. The chief sent the interpreter to me, saying I must order my men to make cartridges and clean their muskets, ready to go on shore in the morning. I assured the interpreter I should give the men no such orders, that they must please themselves. Soon after the chief came on board, threatening to put us all to a cruel death if we refused to obey his orders. For my own part I remained determined, and advised the men not to comply, as I thought by making ourselves useful we should be accounted too valuable. A few hours afterwards he sent to me again, saying, that if myself and the quarter-master would assist them at the great guns, that if also the rest of the men went on shore and succeeded in taking the place, he would then take the money offered for our ransom, and give them twenty dollars for every Chinaman's head they cut off. To these proposals we cheerfully acceded, in hopes of facilitating our deliverance.

"The Mandarin vessels continued firing, having blocked up the entrance of the harbor to prevent the Ladrone boats entering. At this the Ladrones were much exasperated, and about three hundred of them swam on shore, with a short sword lashed close under each arm; they then ran along the banks of the river till they came abreast of the vessels, and then swam off again and boarded them. The Chinese thus attacked, leaped overboard, and endeavored to reach the opposite shore; the Ladrones followed, and cut the greater number of them to pieces in the water. They next towed the vessels out of the harbor, and attacked the town with increased fury. The inhabitants fought about a quarter of an hour, and then retreated to an adjacent hill, from which they were soon driven with great slaughter. After this the Ladrones returned, and plundered the town, every boat leaving it with lading. The Chinese on the hills perceiving most of the boats were off, rallied, and retook the town, killing near two hundred Ladrones. One of my men was unfortunately lost in this dreadful massacre! The Ladrones landed a second time, drove the Chinese out of the town, then reduced it to ashes, and put all their prisoners to death, without regarding either age or sex! I must not omit to mention a most horrid (though ludicrous) circumstance, which happened at this place. The Ladrones were paid by their chief ten dollars for every Chinaman's head they produced. One of my men turning the corner of a street was met by a Ladrone running furiously after a Chinese; he had a drawn sword in his hand, and two Chinaman's heads which he had cut off, tied by their tails, and slung round his neck. I was witness myself to some of them producing five or six to obtain payment!

The Breakup of Madame Ching's Leagues

At the time of Mr. Glasspoole's liberation, the pirates were at the height of their power, attacking imperial Mandarin ships as well as the throne's allies, the Portuguese. Even control of the rivers seemed to rest at their discretion. And yet their formidable association did not survive many months beyond the release of Glasspoole. Though the widow of Ching Yi and the daring Paou were victorious and more powerful than ever, dissensions broke out that soon brought the mighty pirate alliance to an end. A long-standing rivalry with the chief O-po-tae, who commanded one of the flags or divisions of the fleet, came to the fore when O-po-tae disregarded the commands of both Paou and the Chieftainess, refusing to sail to Paou's rescue during a confrontation with a force sent by the Emperor.

Paou, with his bravery and usual good fortune, broke through the blockade, but when he came in contact with O-po-tae, his rage was too violent to be restrained. O-po-tae at first pleaded that his means and strength had been insufficient to do what had been expected of him, but concluded by saying, "Am I bound to come and join the forces of Paou?"

"Would you then separate from us!" cried Paou, more enraged than ever.

O-po-tae answered: "I will not separate myself."

Paou returned "Why then do you not obey the orders of the wife of Ching Yi and my own? What else is this other than separation, that you do not come to assist me when I am surrounded by the enemy? I have sworn it that I will destroy thee, wicked man, that I may do away with this soreness on my back."

The angry words of Paou were followed by others, and

A wood-block illustration portrays the war hunks of the Chinese Ladrones.

then by blows. Paou, though at the moment far inferior in force, first began the fight, and ultimately sustained a sanguinary defeat, and the loss of sixteen vessels. The victors then massacred all their prisoners - three hundred men!

This was the death blow to the confederacy, which had so long defied the Emperor's power, and which might have effected his dethronement. O-po-tae, dreading the vengeance of Paou and his mistress, Ching Yi's widow, whose united forces would have quintupled his own, gained over his men to his views, and proffered a submission to Government, on condition of free pardon, and a proper provision for all.

The petition of the O-po-tai was as follows: After first relating the histories of robbers and rebels who had been pardoned, and even elevated to high positions in Chinese history, O-po-tae concludes that: "There are many instances of such transactions both in former and recent times, by which the country was strengthened, and government increased its power." He then went on to plead that most pirates had little chance to choose another pursuit outside of their crimes:

"We now live in a very populous age; some of us could not agree with their relations, and were driven out like noxious weeds. Some, after having tried all they could, without being able to provide for themselves, at last joined bad society. Some lost their property by shipwrecks; some withdrew into this watery empire to escape from punishment. In such a way those who in the beginning were only three or five, were in the course of time increased to a thousand or ten thousand, and so it went on increasing every year. Would it not have been wonderful if such a multitude, being in want of their daily bread, had not resorted to plunder and robbery to gain their subsistence, since they could not in any other manner be saved from famine? It was from necessity that the laws of the empire were violated, and the merchants robbed of their goods. Being deprived of our land and of our native places, having no house or home to resort to, and relying only on the chances of wind and water, even could we for a moment forget our griefs, we might fall in with a man-of-war, who with stones, darts, and guns, would knock out our brains! Even if we dared to sail up a stream and boldly go on with anxiety of mind under wind, rain, and stormy weather, we must everywhere prepare for fighting. Whether we went to the east, or to the west, and after having felt all the hardships of the sea, the night dew was our only dwelling, and the rude wind our meal.

But now we will avoid these perils, leave our connections, and desert our comrades; we will make our submission."

Finally, he added a little flattery: "The power of Government knows no bounds; it reaches to the islands in the sea, and every man is afraid, and sighs. Oh we must be destroyed by our crimes, none can escape who oposeth the laws of Government. May you then feel compassion for those who are deserving of death; may you sustain us by your humanity!"

The Government that had made so many lamentable displays of its weakness, was glad to make an unreal parade of its mercy. It was but too happy to grant all the conditions instantly, and, in the fulsome language of its historians, "feeling that compassion is the way of heaven - that it is the right way to govern by righteousness - it therefore redeemed these pirates from destruction, and pardoned their former crimes."

O-po-tae, however, had hardly struck his free flag, and his band of eight thousand pirates were hardly in the power of the Chinese, when it was proposed by many that they should all be treacherously murdered. The governor happened to be more honorable and humane, or probably, only more politic than those who made this foul proposal - he knew that such a bloody breach of faith would forever prevent the pirates still in arms from voluntary submitting; he knew equally well, even weakened as they were by O-po-tae's defection, that the Government could not reduce them by force, and he thought by keeping his faith with them, he might turn the force of those who had submitted against those who still held out, and so destroy the pirates with the pirates. Consequently the men were allowed to remain uninjured, and their leader, O-po-tae, having changed his name to that of Hoe-been, or "The Lustre of Instruction," was elevated to the rank of an imperial officer.

Madame Ching and Paou continued for some months to pillage the coast, and to beat the Chinese and the Mandarins' troops and ships, and seemed almost as strong as before the separation of O-po-tae's flag. But that example of O-po-tae was probably operating in the minds of many of the outlaws, and finally the lawless heroine herself, who was the spirit that kept the complicated body together.

A rumor of her intentions having reached shore, the Mandarin sent off a certain Chow, a doctor of Macao known to Paou. The doctor explained, and assured the chief, that if he would submit, the Government was inclined to treat him far more favorably and more honorably than O-po-tae. But if he continued to resist, the coast and the rivers would be armed and O-po-tae sent to fight against him. Their conversation, and the good doctor's powers of flattery, were recorded as thus:

Fei-heung-Chow: "Friend Paou, do you know why I come to you?"

Paou: "Thou hast committed some crime and comest to me for protection?"

Chow: "By no means."

Paou: "You will then know how it stands concerning the report about our submission, if it is true or false?"

Chow: "You are again wrong here, Sir. What are you in comparison with O-po-tae?"

Paou: "Who is bold enough to compare me with O-po-tae?"

Chow: "I know very well that O-po-tae could not come up to you, Sir; but I mean only, that since O-po-tae has made his submission, since he has got his pardon and been created a Government officer, how would it be, if you with your whole crew should also submit, and if his Excellency should desire to treat you in the same manner, and to give you the same rank as O-po-tae? Your submission would produce more joy to Government than the submission of O-po-tae. You should not wait for wisdom to act wisely; you should make up your mind to submit to the Government with all your followers. I will assist you in every respect, it would be the means of securing your own happiness and the lives of all your adherents."

Chang-paou remained like a statue without motion, and Fei-heung Chow went on to say: "You should think about this affair in time, and not stay till the last moment. Is it not clear that O-po-tae, since you could not agree together, has joined Government. He being enraged against you, will fight, united with the forces of the Government, for your destruction; and who could help you, so that you might overcome your enemies? If O-po-tae could before vanquish you quite alone, how much more can he now when he is united with Government? O-po-tae will then satisfy his hatred against you, and you yourself will soon be taken either at Wei-chow or at Neaou-chow. If the merchant-vessels of Hwy-chaou, the boats of Kwang-chow, and all the fishing vessels, unite together to surround and attack you in the open sea, you will certainly have enough to do. But even supposing they should not attack you, you will soon feel the want of provisions to sustain you and all your followers. It is always wisdom to provide before things happen; stupidity and folly to never think about future events. It is too late to reflect upon events when things have happened; you should, therefore, consider this matter in time!"

Paou was puzzled, but after being closeted for some time with his mistress, Madame Ching, who gave her high permission for him to make arrangements with Doctor Chow, he said he would repair with his fleet to the Bocca Tigris, and there communicate personally with the organs of Government.

After two visits had been paid to the pirate-fleets by two inferior Mandarins, who carried the Imperial proclamation of free pardon, and who, at the order of Madame Ching, were treated to a sumptuous banquet by Paou, the Governor-general of the province went himself in one vessel to the pirates' ships. As the governor approached, the pirates hoisted their flags, played on their instruments, and fired their guns, so that the smoke rose in clouds, and then bent sail to meet him. On this the dense population that were ranged thousands after thousands along the shore, to witness the important reconciliation, became sorely alarmed, and the Governor-general seems to have had a strong inclination to run away. But in a brief space of time, the long dreaded Madame Ching, supported by her Lieutenant Paou, and followed by three other of her principal commanders, mounted the side of the governor's ship, and rushed through the smoke to the spot where his Excellency was stationed; where they fell on their hands and knees, shed tears, knocked their heads on the deck before him, and received his gracious pardon, and promise for future kind treatment. They then withdrew satisfied, having promised to give in a list of their ships, and of all else they possessed, within three days.

But the sudden apparition of some large Portuguese ships, and some Government war-junks, made the pirates suspect treachery. They immediately set sail, and the negotiations were interrupted for several days.

They were at last concluded by the boldness of their female leader. "If the Governor-general," said this heroine, "a man of the highest rank, could come to us quite alone, why should not I go to the officers of Government? If there be danger in it, I take it all on myself; no person among you need trouble himself about me - my mind is made up, and I will go to Canton!"

Paou said, "If the widow of Ching Yi goes, we must fix a time for her return. If this pass without our obtaining any information, we must collect all our forces, and go before Canton. This is my opinion as to what ought to be done; comrades, let me hear yours!"

The pirates, then, struck with the intrepidity of their chieftainess, and loving her more than ever, answered, "Friend Paou, we have heard thy opinion, but we think it better to wait for the news here, on the water, than to send the wife of Ching Yi alone to be killed." Nor would they allow her to leave the fleet.

Matters were in this state of indecision, when the two inferior Mandarins who had before visited the pirates, ventured out to repeat their visit. These officers protested no treachery had been intended, and pledged themselves, that if the widow of Ching Yi would repair to the Governor, she would be kindly received, and everything settled to their hearts' satisfaction.

With this, in the language of our old ballads, Madame Ching spoke out: "You say well, gentlemen! and I will go myself to Canton with some other of our ladies, accompanied by you!" And accordingly she and a number of the pirates' wives with their children, went fearlessly to Canton, arranged everything, and found they had not been deceived. The fleet soon followed. On its arrival every vessel was supplied with pork and with wine, and every man (in lieu it may be supposed, of his share of the vessels, and plundered property he resigned) received at the same time a bill for a certain quantity of money. Those who wished it, could join the military force of Government for pursuing the remaining pirates; and those who objected, dispersed and withdrew into the country.

The valiant Paou, following the example of his rival O-po-tae, entered into the service of Government, and proceeded against such of his former associates and friends as would not accept the pardon offered them. There was some hard fighting, but the two renegades successively conquered the remaining pirate leaders - the chief Shih Url, styled "The scourge of the Eastern Ocean" was forced to surrender himself; "Frog's Meal," another dreadful pirate, fled to Manila, and within a few months all the "wasps of the ocean" were destroyed or dissipated.

Madame Ching settled in Canton, a rich woman. She kept a gambling house, and bore Paou a son, leading a respectable life until her death in 1844 at the age of sixty-nine.

Another Dragon Lady

Another Chinese dragon lady gets brief mention in The History of Piracy by Philip Gosse:

"Although no other woman pirate in all history reached so high a pitch of glory and renown as the widow Ching, it would be unfair to the memory of another, more recent, widow, Mrs. Hon-cho-lo, to pass her by in silence. Mrs. Lo, like Mrs. Ching, was married to a pirate and on his death, as recently as 1921, took over command of his fleet. She soon struck terror into the countryside round about Pakhoi, where she carried on the best traditions of the craft as admiral of some sixty ocean-going junks. Although both young and pretty, she had a reputation for being a thorough-going murderess and pirate.

During the late revolution Mrs. Lo joined forces with General Wong-min-tong and received the rank of full colonel. After the war she resumed her piracies, occasionally for the sake of vanity surprising and plundering a village or two, from which she usually carried away some fifty or sixty girls to sell.

Her short but brilliant career ended quite suddenly in October 1922.

Even today Pakhoi, or Beihai, in Southeastern China is known as a harbor for modern-day pirates. China's chief pearl grounds are nearby, and the city is an important fishing and trade port on the Gulf of Tonkin.

Pirate's crimes often included the unspeakable abuse of women found passenger upon plundered ships. This woodblock print was used to illustrate the helpless fate of English women aboard a ship detained by Benito de Soto in the *Pirates Own Book*.

Captive Among Pirates

Many of the tales surrounding women who fell in with pirates were edited for the puritan sentiments of the time, most concluding that their treatment was simply too horrible to relate. For instance, in a long confession from the captured Pirate Captain Charles Gibbs, a tale is told of a young woman who is spared the butchering her shipmates receive, only to suffer far worse. In the *Pirates Own Book*, the following tale was told:

"An instance of the most barbarous and cold blooded murder of which the wretched Gibbs gives an account in the course of his confessions, is that of an innocent and beautiful female of about 17 or 18 years of age! She was with her parents, a passenger on board a Dutch ship, bound from Curracoa to Holland; there were a number of other passengers, male and female, on board, all of whom except the young lady above-mentioned were put to death. Her unfortunate parents were inhumanly butchered before her eyes, and she was doomed to witness the agonies and to hear the expiring, heart-piercing groans of those whom she held most dear, and on whom she depended for protection! The life of their wretched daughter was spared for the most nefarious purposes - she was taken by the pirates to the west end of Cuba, where they had a rendezvous, with a small fort that mounted four guns - here she was confined about two months, and where, as has been said by the murderer Gibbs, "she received such treatment, the bare recollection of which causes me to shudder!" At the expiration of the two months she was taken by the pirates on board of one of their vessels, and among whom a consultation was soon after held, which resulted in the conclusion that it would be necessary for their own personal safety to put her to death! She was poisoned and, upon her death, her lifeless body was then committed to the deep. Gibbs persists in his declaration that in this horrid transaction he took no part, that such was his pity for this poor ill-fated female, that he interceded for her life so long as he could do it with safety to his own!

An account of Benito de Soto, a pirate executed in Gibraltar in 1830, illustrates the expected fate of women caught on board captured ships. De Soto's crimes were recounted in the *Pirates Own Book*, among them the telling fate of a ship full of civilians aboard the Morning Star, a British ship that fell victim to de Soto in 1828. The Morning Star was enough from Ceylon to England, bearing cargo along with several passengers including a major and his wife, an assistant surgeon, two civilians, 25 invalid soldiers, and three or four of their wives. De Soto's men gained an easy surrender of the British ship, then detained her while they relieved it of cargo, and feasted upon her stores, particularly the strong drink. What men survived the initial attack were put to work assisting the pirates in their endeavors, or detained in chains above board. The women, held below, were badly abused, their screams reaching the ears of the helpless men above board.

Before leaving the ship, the women were locked within a cabin and heavy lumber was heaped on the hatches. The men were left chained on the deck, and before abandoning the ship, the pirates bored holes in the planks of the vessel below the surface of the water in order to sink it. The women forced their way on deck and freed the men who, after the pirates had sailed a safe distance, set the pumps to work and managed to keep their now un-navigable boat afloat until they were rescued the following day by a passing vessel.

A Child Bride Turned Crook

An account of pirates and trade along the Indian Coast was given by Colonel John Biddulph in 1907. In *The Pirates of Malabar and An Englishwoman in India*, Biddulph relates the tale of one woman's ill fate in the region, and her apparent gradual transformation from innocent victim to determined plunderer. His story was as follows:

Long after they had disappeared from the seas to the West, the Indian trade continued to be exposed to the ravages of native pirates, who were not finally coerced into good behavior until well into the nineteenth century. The early records of the East India Company furnished the account of Mrs. Gyfford, from her first arrival in India until her final disappearance in the Court of Chancery, showing the vicissitudes and dangers to which an Englishwoman in India was exposed two hundred years ago.

It is useful to consider the difference in the men sent out by England to the East and West Indies during the seventeenth and part of the eighteenth centuries. To the West Indies went out representatives of the landed gentry from every county in England. Charters were obtained from the Crown, conferring estates and sometimes whole islands, on men of ancient families. Slaves were cheap, and sugar cultivation brought in great wealth. The whole machinery of English life was reproduced in the tropics - counties, parishes, sheriffs, rectories, tithes, an established church, etc.

The same causes that sent the Cavaliers to Virginia sent a smaller migration to the West Indies. At the Restoration, the men who had conquered Jamaica for Cromwell were unwilling to return to England. Monmouth's rebellion and the expulsion of the Stuarts produced a fresh influx. But, whether

75

Cavaliers or Roundheads or Jacobites, they came from the landholding class in England.

In the East Indies nothing of the kind was possible. The acquisition of land for agriculture was out of the question. Trade was the only opening, and that was monopolized by the Company. Except as a servant of the Company, an Englishman had no legal status in the East. The chief profits went to the shareholders in London. If at the end of twenty-five years or so a Company's servant could return to England with money made by private trade, he was a fortunate man. Private traders and a few of the governors were alone able to make fortunes. The result was that the men who went to India were of a totally different class from those who went to America and the West Indies. They were young men from small trading families in London, Greenwich, and Deptford, or from seaport towns like Bristol and Plymouth. Among them were some restless and adventurous spirits who found life in England too tame or too burdensome. For such men, India was long regarded as a useful outlet.

A Bombay pay-list of January, 1716, shows us the official salaries at that time. The Governor received £300 per annum. Next to him came eight merchants, who with him constituted the Council, and received respectively, one £100, one £70, two £50, and four £40 each. Below them came three senior factors at £30 each, three junior factors at £15, and seven writers at £5. The tale is completed by the accountant and the chaplain, who received £100 each. A writer on entering the service had to find security for £500, which was increased to £1000 when he rose to be a factor. The unmarried servants of the Company were lodged at the Company's expense; the married ones received a lodging allowance, and a public table was maintained. In fact, the Company treated them as if they were apprentices in a warehouse in St. Paul's Churchyard, and, when the conditions of their service are taken into account, it is not surprising that there was a considerable amount of dishonesty among them.

Catherine Cooke

On March 9th, 1709, the Loyall Bliss, East Indiaman under the command of Captain Hudson, left the Downs and sailed for Bengal. As passengers, she carried Captain Gerard Cooke, his wife, a son, and two daughters, together with a few soldiers. Cooke was now returning to Bengal as engineer with the rank of captain. The Loyall Bliss made slow progress, rounding the Cape in August under continuing contrary winds and bad weather. By mid-September, the southwest monsoon, on which they depended to carry them up the bay, had ceased to blow, supplies were low, and the passengers were suffering ill tempers and health.

In October they anchored again under the guns of the Portuguese fort on the island of Angediva, where the chief of the East India Company's factory at Carwar was Mr. John Harvey. Harvey entertained Captain Hudson and all the gentlemen and ladies on board "in a splendid manner." To Mr. Harvey and the Company's officials they were welcome as they brought the latest news from England. And Mr. John Harvey found other matters of interest in his visitors. There were few Englishwomen in India in those days, and the unexpected advent of a fresh young English girl aroused his susceptibilities to such an extent that he forgot to report to Bombay the arrival of the Loyall Bliss, for which he, in due time, received a reprimand. He quickly made known to Captain Cooke that he had taken a very great liking to his eldest daughter.

Mistress Catherine Cooke, "a most beautiful lady, not exceeding thirteen or fourteen years of age." Cooke was a poor man, and had left two more daughters in England. Mr. Harvey offered to make great settlements provided the Father and Mother would consent to her marriage, and Mistress Catherine Cooke, to oblige her parents, consented.

There was little time for delay, as the captain of the Loyall Bliss was impatient to be off. The Company's ship, Tankerville, was on the coast, bound southward, and it was desirable they should sail in company for mutual protection. So, after about two weeks ashore, the crew of the Loyall Bliss made sail for Bengal, leaving behind the young bride at Carwar.

To the lookers-on the marriage was repugnant, and can hardly have been a happy one for the young girl, as Harvey was a deformed man and in years. He had been long on the coast, and by diligent trading had acquired a little money; but he had other things to think of besides his private trade, as we find recorded at the time that the Rajah of Carwar continues ill-natured. By the end of 1710, he made up his mind to resign the Company's service, wind up his affairs, and go to England; so Mr. Robert Mence was appointed to succeed him at Carwar, and, in April, 1711, Harvey and his child-wife came to Bombay. But to wind up trading transactions of many years' standing was necessarily a long business, and there was no necessity for hurry, as no ship could leave for England till after the monsoon.

As always happened in those days, his own accounts were mixed up with those of the Company, and would require laborious disentanglement. Before leaving Carwar, he had leased to the Company his trading ship, the Salamander, and had taken the precaution to pay himself out of the Company's treasure chest at Carwar. Before long, there was an order to the Carwar chief to recharge Mr. Harvey 402 Pagodas, 17 Jett, and 4 Pice he had charged to the Company for the use of the Salamander, the account having been liquidated in Bombay; from which it would appear that he had been paid twice for his ship. The accounts of those days must have been maddening affairs owing to the multiplicity of coinages. Pounds sterling, Pagodas, Rupees, Fanams, Xeraphims, Laris, Juttals, Matte, Reis, Rials, Cruzadoes, Sequins, Pice, Budgerooks, and Dollars of different values were all brought into the official accounts. In 1718, the confusion was increased by a tin coinage called Deccanees. The conversion of sums from one coinage to another, many of them of unstable value, must have been an everlasting trouble. In August we find Harvey writing to the Council to say that he had at Tellicherry a chest of pillar dollars weighing over 289 pounds, which he requests may be paid into the Company's cash there, and in return a chest of dollars may be given him at Bombay.

His young wife doubtless assisted him in his complicated accounts, and gained some knowledge of local trade. It must have been a wonderful delight to her to escape from the dullness of Carwar and mix in the larger society of Bombay, and she must have realized with sadness the mistake she had made in marrying a deformed man old enough to be her grandfather, at the solicitation of her parents. She made, at this time, two acquaintances that were destined to have considerable influence on her future life. On August 5th, the Godolphin, twenty-one days from Mocha, approached Bombay, but being unable to make the harbor before nightfall, anchored outside; a proceeding that would appear, even to a landsman, absolutely suicidal in the middle of the monsoon, but was probably due to fear of pirates. That night heavy weather came on, the ship's cable parted, and the Godolphin became a total wreck at the foot of Malabar Hill. Apparently, all the Englishmen on board were saved, among them a young man named Thomas Chown, who lost all his possessions. There was also in Bombay, at the time, a young factor, William Gyfford, who had come to India six years before as a writer, at the age of seventeen. We shall hear of both of them again.

News of the death of Mr. Robert Mence at Carwar came in October. "Tho his time there was so small we find he had misapplied 1700 and odd pagodas to his own use," the Bombay Council reported to the Directors in London. In his place was appointed Mr. Miles Fleetwood, who was then in Bombay awaiting a passage to the Persian Gulf where he had been appointed a factor. Harvey and his wife returned with him to Carwar, Harvey to adjust some depending accounts with the country people there. Four months after his return to Carwar, Harvey died, leaving Catherine a widow.

She remained at Carwar, engaged in winding up the trading affairs of her late husband, and asserting her claim to his estate, which had been taken possession of by the Company's officials, according to custom. According to the practice of the day, every merchant and factor had private trading accounts, which were mixed up with the Company's accounts, so that on retirement they were not allowed to leave the country till the Company's claims were settled. In case of death, their estates were taken possession of for the same reason.

Husband Number Two

Two months later, Mr. Thomas Chown was sent down to Carwar as a factor, and, a few weeks after his arrival, he married the young widow. Application was now made to the Council at Bombay for the effects of her late husband to be made over to her, and orders were sent to Carwar for the late Mr. Harvey's effects to be sold, and one-third of the estate to be

80

paid to Mrs. Chown, provided Harvey had died intestate. The Carwar factor chief replied that the effects had realized 13,146 rupees 1 fanam and 12 budgerooks; that Harvey had left a will dated the April 8th, 1708, and that therefore nothing had been paid to Mrs. Chown. It was necessary for Chown and his wife to go to Bombay and prosecute their claims in person. The short voyage was destined to be an eventful one.

On November 3, 1712, Chown and Catherine left Carwar in the Anne ketch, having a cargo of pepper and wax on board, to urge their claim to the late Mr. Harvey's estate. The coast swarmed with pirate craft, among which those of Conajee Angria were the most numerous and the most formidable. It was usual, therefore, for every cargo of any value to be convoyed by an armed vessel. To protect the Anne, Governor Aislabie's armed yacht had been sent down, and a small frigate, the Defiance, was also with them. The day after leaving Carwar they were swooped down upon by four of Angria's ships, and a hot action ensued. The brunt of it fell on the Governor's yacht, which had both masts shot away and was forced to surrender. The ketch tried to escape back to Carwar, but was laid aboard by two grabs, and had to surrender when she had expended most of her ammunition.

In the action, Chown had his arm torn off by a cannonshot, and expired in his wife's arms. So again, in little more than three years from her first marriage, Catherine was left a widow when she could hardly have been eighteen. The captured vessels and the prisoners were carried off; the crews to Gheriah and the European prisoners to Colaba. To make matters worse for the poor widow, she was expecting the birth of an infant.

Great was the excitement in Bombay when the news of Catherine's capture arrived. The Governor was away at Surat, and all that could be done was to address Angria; so a letter was written to him asking for the captives and all papers to be restored, and some medicine was sent for the wounded. After keeping them a month in captivity, Angria sent back his prisoners, except the captain's ransom. In acknowledgment of kindness shown to the released prisoners by the Seedee, that chief was presented with a pair of Musquetoons, a fowling-piece, and five yards of embossed cloth. But in the Governor's absence the Council could do nothing about payment of ransom. When he returned, negotiations went on through the European prisoners in Colaba. Angria being sincerely anxious for peace with the English while he was in arms against his own chief, terms were arranged, and Lieutenant Mackintosh was dispatched to Colaba with ransom money for the Europeans. He returned on February 22, 1713, bringing with him Catherine and the other captives, the captured goods, and the Anne ketch. The yacht was too badly damaged to put to sea and, according to Downing, Catherine was in such a state that Mackintosh, "was obliged to wrap his clothes about her to cover her nakedness." Yet "she most courageously withstood all Angria's base usage, and endured his insults beyond expectation."

Shortly afterwards she was delivered of a son. Out of her first husband's estate one thousand rupees were granted her for present necessities, with an allowance of one hundred xeraphims a month.

Husband Number Three

Very shortly afterwards we find her being married for the third time, to young William Gyfford, with the Governor's approval. According to the statute law of Bombay, no marriage was binding, except if it had the Governor's consent; Hamilton tells us how on one occasion a factor, Mr. Solomon

Lloyd, married a young lady without the Governor's consent. Sir John Gayer dissolved the marriage, and married the lady again to his own son.

In October, two and a half years after her first husband's death, seven thousand four hundred and ninety-two rupees, being one-third of his estate, were paid over to Catherine. It is carefully recorded that neither of her deceased husbands had left wills, though the existence of Harvey's will had been very precisely recorded by the Council fifteen months before. Young Gyfford, who was then twenty-five, appears to have been a favorite with the Governor, and had lately been given charge of the Bombay Market. Eighteen months after his marriage, we find William Gyfford appointed supercargo of the Catherine, trading to Mocha. The office was a most desirable one for a young factor. It afforded him opportunities for private trade at first hand, instead of through agents, that in the mind of an adventurous young man quite outbalanced the perils of the sea.

In spite of small salaries, a goodly public appearance was made by the Company's servants. At the public table, where they sat in order of seniority, all dishes, plates, and drinking-cups were of pure silver or fine china. English, Portuguese, and Indian cooks were employed, so that every taste might be suited. Before and after meals silver basins were taken round for each person to wash his hands. Arrack, Shiraz wine, and "pale punch," a compound of brandy, rose-water, lime-juice, and sugar, were drunk, and, at times, we hear of Canary wine.

On festival days the Governor would invite the whole factory to a picnic in some garden outside the city. On such an occasion, a procession was formed, headed by the Governor and his lady, in palanquins. Two large ensigns were carried before them, followed by a number of lead horses in gorgeous trappings of velvet and silver. Following the Governor came the Captain of the Peons on horseback, with forty or fifty armed men on foot. Next followed the members of the Council, the merchants, factors, and writers, in order of seniority, in fine bullock coaches or riding on horses, all maintained at the company's expense. At the Dewallee festival every servant of the Company, from the Governor to the youngest writer, received a "peshcush" from the brokers and bunyas, which to the younger men were of much importance; as they depended on these gifts to procure their annual supply of clothes.

Of the country itself, away from the coast, they were profoundly ignorant. They talked of the people as Gentoos, Moors, Mallwans, Sanganians, Gennims, Warrels, Coulis, Patanners, etc., and the number of political, racial, religious, and linguistic divisions presented to their view must have been especially puzzling. Owing to the numerous languages necessary to carry on trade on the Malabar coast, they were forced to depend almost entirely on untrustworthy Portuguese interpreters.

After two years' work, as supercargo on different ships, Gyfford was sent down to Anjengo as chief of the factory. Anjengo was at that time one of the most important factories on the Malabar coast, though of comparatively recent establishment. It was first frequented by the Portuguese who, after a time, were ousted by the Dutch. It belonged to the Rani Ashure of Attinga, a woman who owned a small principality extending along sixty miles of coast. In 1688, the Rani invited the English to form a trading settlement in her dominions, and two were formed, at Vittoor (Returah) and Villanjuen (Brinjone). But for some reason, she became dissatisfied with the English, and the hostility of the Dutch, in spite of the alliance between the two countries in Europe, caused great trouble. In November, 1693, John Brabourne was sent to Attinga, where, by his successful diplomacy, the sandy spit of Anjengo was granted to the English, as a site for a fort, together with the monopoly of the pepper trade of Attinga. Soon, the Dutch protests and intrigues aroused the Rani's suspicions. She ordered Brabourne to stop his building. Finding him deaf to her orders, she first tried to starve out the English by cutting off supplies, but as the sea was open, the land blockade proved ineffectual. She then sent an armed force against Brabourne, which was speedily put to flight, and terms of peace were arranged. The fort was completed, and a most flourishing trade in pepper and cotton cloth speedily grew up. Anjengo became the first port of call for outward-bound ships.

In June, 1717, William Gyfford was appointed a chief of the Anjengo settlement as soon as the monsoon would permit. So, in due course of time, Gyfford and Catherine went to Anjengo where Gyfford threw himself into the pepper trade for his own betterment, using the Company's money for his own purposes, and joined hands with the Portuguese interpreter, Ignatio Malheiros, who appears to have been a consummate rogue. Malheiros seems to have enraged locals by obtaining possession of some pagoda land in a money-lending transaction. Gyfford also aroused resentment by trying to cheat the native traders over the price of pepper, by showing fictitious entries in the factory books, and by the use of false weights. The only thing wanting for an explosion was the alienation of the Mahommedan section, which, before long, was produced by chance and by Gyfford's folly.

It happened that some Mahommedan traders came to the fort to transact business with Cowse, who had resumed business as a private merchant. Finding he was not available, they went to the interpreter's house, to sit down and wait. While there, the interpreter's "strumpet" threw some hooli powder on one of the merchants. Stung by the insult, the man drew his sword, wounded the woman, and would have killed her, if he and his companions had not been disarmed.

Gyfford, when they were brought before him, allowed himself to be influenced by the interpreter, and ordered them to be turned out of the fort, after their swords had been insultingly broken over their heads. The people of Attinga flew to arms, and threatened the fort. For some months there were constant skirmishes. The English had no difficulty in defeating all attacks, but nonetheless trade was brought to a standstill.

Bombay sent an emissary and a peace was negotiated. Things having quieted down, Gyfford was flush with hopes of "Peace and Pepper," and devoted himself to trade. He had at this time a brigantine called the Thomas, commanded by Catherine's brother, Thomas Cooke, doing his private trade along the coast. The year 1720 passed quietly. Force having proved unavailing, the Attinga people dissembled their anger, and waited for an opportunity to revenge themselves. So well was the popular feeling against the English concealed, that Cowse, with his long experience and knowledge of the language, had no suspicions.

Widowed Once Again

There had been an old custom, since the establishment of the factory, of giving presents yearly to the Rani, in the name of the Company; but for some years the practice had fallen into abeyance. Gyfford, wishing to ingratiate himself with the authorities, resolved to revive the custom, and to do so in the most ceremonious way, by going himself with the presents. Accordingly, on April 11, 1721, accompanied by all the

86

merchants and factors, and taking all his best men, about one hundred and twenty in number, and the same number of coolies, Gyfford started for Attinga, four miles up the river. An enormous crowd received them, seeming friendly. The details of what followed are imperfectly recorded, and much is left to conjecture, but Gyfford's foolish over-confidence is sufficiently apparent. In spite of their brave display, his men carried no ammunition. Poola Venjamutta was not to be seen. They were told he was drunk, and they must wait till he was fit to receive them. He was apparently playing a double part, but the blame for what followed was afterwards laid on his rival, Poola Cadamon Pillay. Cowse's suspicions were aroused, and he advised an immediate return to Anjengo, but Gyfford refused to take the advice. He is said to have struck Cowse, and to have threatened him with imprisonment. The Rani also sent a message, advising a return to Anjengo. It was getting late, and to extricate himself from the crowd, Gyfford allowed the whole party to be inveigled into a small enclosure. To show his goodwill to the crowd, he ordered his men to fire a salvo, and then he found that the ammunition carried by the coolies had been secured, and they were defenseless. In this hopeless position, he managed to entrust a letter to the hands of a friendly native. It reached Anjengo at one o'clock the next day, and ran as follows:

"Captain Sewell. We are treacherously dealt with here, therefore keep a very good look-out of any designs on you. Have a good look to your two Trankers (palisades). We hope to be with you tonight. Take care and don't frighten the women; we are in no great danger. Give the bearer a Chequeen."

But none of the English were to see Anjengo again. That night, or the next morning, a sudden attack was made, the crowd surged in on the soldiers, overwhelmed them, and cut them to pieces. The principal English were seized and reserved for a more cruel death. In the confusion, Cowse, who was a favorite among the natives, managed to disguise himself, got through the crowd, and sought to reach Anjengo by a little frequented path. By bad luck he was overtaken by a Mahommedan merchant who owed him money. Cowse offered to acquit him of the debt, but to no purpose. He was mercilessly killed, and thus the debt was settled. The rest of the English were tortured to death, Gyfford and the interpreter being reserved for the worst barbarities. Ignatio Malheiros was gradually dismembered, while Gyfford had his tongue torn out, was nailed to a log of wood, and sent floating down the river.

It is easy to picture to one's self the consternation in Anjengo, that April 12th, when, soon after midday, Gyfford's hasty note was received, and the same evening, when a score of wounded men straggled in to confirm the worst fears; all of them miserably wounded, some with twelve or thirteen cuts and arrows in their bodies.

Gyfford had taken away all the able men with him, leaving in the fort less than forty old men, boys, and pensioners. At their head were Robert Sewell, who describes himself as Storekeeper, Captain and Adjutant by order of Governor Boone; Lieutenant Peter Lapthorne, Ensign Thomas Davis, and Gunner Samuel Ince. The first three of them were absolutely useless, and Gunner Ince, whose name deserves to be remembered, was the only one of the four who rose to the situation. His first care was for the three English women, whose husbands had just been killed. By good fortune there happened to be in the road a small country ship that had brought a consignment of cowries from the Maldives. Catherine, for the third time a widow, Mrs. Cowse with four children, and Mrs. Burton with two, were hastily put on board, and sailed at once for Madras. No mention appears of Catherine having any children with her, but she carried off the factory records and papers, and what money she could lay her hands on. She was no longer the confiding girl, who had given herself to Governor Harvey eleven years before. She had learned something of the world she lived in, and intended to take care of herself as well as she could. She even tried to carry off Peter Lapthorne with her, but Sewell intervened and prevented it. So giving him hasty directions to act as her agent, she passed through the dangerous Anjengo surf and got on board. A letter to her from Lapthorne, written a few weeks later, relates that the only property he could find belonging to her were "two wigs and a bolster and some opium" in the warehouse.

Sewell and his companions set to work to hold the fort against the innevitable attack, and to bring in the warehouse goods and employee effects for protection. An urgent appeal was sent to Calicut. The surgeon had been killed with Gyfford; they had no smith or carpenter or tools, except a few hatchets. The Attinga people swarming into Anjengo burned and plundered the settlement, forcing a crowd of women and children to take refuge in the small fort. Though no concerted attack was made at first, the assailants tried with fire arrows to set fire to the palm-leaf roofs, which had to be dismantled, exposing all to the burning rays of a tropical sun or the torrential rains of the monsoon. The siege lasted six months, as intelligence of the disaster did not reach Bombay till the beginning of July and, as the monsoon was in full force, assistance could not be sent until October.

Mr. Midford, who arrived with three hundred men reported that the safety of the fort had been entirely due to Gunner Ince. Sewell and Lapthorne had set the example of plundering the Company, and their men had done as much damage as the enemy. Sewell, as storekeeper, had no books, and said he never had kept any. Lapthorne had retained two months' pay, due to the men killed with Gyfford, and asserted his right to it. Much of the Company's treasure was unaccounted for, and Mrs. Catherine Gyfford had carried off the books. Midford sent Sewell and Lapthorne under arrest to Bombay, where they were let off with a scolding, and proceeded to restore order. The Rani and Venjamutta were friendly, but told him he must take his own vengeance on the Nairs for their inhuman action. So he commenced a series of raids into the surrounding country, which reduced it to some sort of subjection. A cessation of arms was patched up, and Midford installed himself as chief.

Midford proved to be no more honest than his predecessors. He monopolized the pepper trade on his own private account, making himself advances out of the Company's treasury. But that is another story.

Escape with a Rogue Commodore

We left Mrs. Gyfford flying from Anjengo in a small country ship, with two other English women and six children. The misery that the three poor widows must have endured for a month, crowded into a small country boat, without preparation or ordinary comforts, at the hottest time of the year, must have been extreme. On the May 17th, the fugitives landed at Madras.

The Council there granted them a compassionate allowance, of which Catherine refused to avail herself. After a time she made her way to Calcutta and joined her father's family, leaving, with an agent in Madras, the Anjengo factory books, which, after repeated demands, were surrendered to the Madras Council. From Madras to Calcutta she was pursued by the demands of the Bombay Council. The books had been restored at Madras, and the Bengal Government extracted Rs.7312 from her; but, in reply to further demands, she would only answer that she was "an unfortunate widow, struggling with adversity, whose husband had met his death serving our Honourable Masters," and that it was shameful to demand money from her when she herself was owed large sums by the Company. She could only refer them to her agents at Madras and Anjengo. Still, she was in a considerable dilemma, as she could not get out of the country without a full settlement of accounts, and, if resistance was carried too far, her father might be made to suffer.

At this juncture an unexpected way of escape presented itself. Twelve months before this, Commodore Matthews had arrived in Bombay with a squadron of the Royal Navy for the suppression of piracy. But Matthews was more bent on enriching himself by trade than on harrying pirates; and as his own trading was inimical to the Company's interests and certain to set the Company's servants against him, he had from the first assumed a position of hostility to the Company. He seized every opportunity to damage the Company's interests and lower the Company's authority. All who were in the Company's bad books found a patron and protector in Matthews.

So when Matthew's flagship appeared in September, 1722, Catherine was quick to grasp the opportunity that presented itself of bidding defiance to her pursuers. She at once opened communication with Matthews, and besought his protection. She was an unfortunate widow who had lost two husbands by violent deaths in the Company's service, and, now that she was unprotected, the Company was trying to wring from her the little money she had brought away from Anjengo, while she herself had large claims against the Company. This was quite enough for Matthews. Here was a young and pretty woman with a good sum of money, shamefully persecuted by the Company, toward which he felt nothing but hostility. At one stroke he could gratify his dislike of the Company and succor a badly treated young woman, whose hard fate should arouse sympathy in every generous mind; so the Bengal Council were told that Mrs. Gyfford was now under the protection of the Crown, and was not to be molested.

In the hope of securing some portion of the money due to the Company, the Council attached the brigantine Thomas, commanded by Mrs. Gyfford's brother. A letter was at once forthcoming from Matthews to say that he had purchased Mrs. Gyfford's interest in the vessel. Finding themselves thus forestalled, the Council begged Matthews not to take her away from Calcutta till she had furnished security for the Company's claim of Rs.50,000. Matthews replied that he should take her to Bombay, where she would answer anything that might be alleged against her. As soon as he had completed his trading in Bengal, Catherine, with her effects, embarked on board the Lyon, and so returned to Bombay. There, in January, 1723, we find her living under Matthews' roof, much to the wrath of the Council and the scandal of her former acquaintances. By this time, the Council had received from Anjengo more precise details as to what was due to the Company from Gyfford's estate. All the cowries, pepper, and cloth that were said to belong to Gyfford had been bought with the Company's money, and the Company's claim against his estate was nearly £9000. A stringent order was sent to Mrs. Gyfford, forbidding her to leave Bombay till the claim was settled. Matthews at once put her on board the Lyon again, and there she remained; not venturing to set foot on shore, lest the Council should lay hands on her.

By the end of the year, Matthews was ready to return to

England. Intent to the last on trade, he touched at Carwar, Tellicherry, and St. David's, and, in Catherine's interests, a visit was also paid Anjengo to try and recover some of the property she claimed to have left there. She was not going to be put off with Lapthorne's "two wigs and a bolster." In July, 1724, the Lyon reached Portsmouth, and was put out of commission.

At first the Directors appear to have paid little attention to Catherine, perhaps not thinking her worth powder and shot. Their principal anger was directed against Matthews, against whom they obtained a decree in the Court of Chancery for unlawful trading. But Catherine would not keep silence. Perhaps she really believed in the justice of her claims. She bombarded the Directors with petitions, till at last, two years after her arrival in England, they tardily awoke to the fact that they themselves had substantial claims against her. They offered to submit the claims to arbitration, to which Mrs. Gyfford consented; but as she still refrained from coming to close quarters, they filed a suit against her in the Court of Chancery, nearly four years after her arrival in England. Mrs. Gyfford promptly replied with a counter-suit, in which, among other things, she claimed £10,000 for presents taken by Gyfford to the Rani of Attinga on that fatal April 11, seven years before. Four years later, she was still deep in litigation, having quarreled with her agent, Peter Lapthorne, among others.

Here we may say goodbye to her. For those who are curious in such matters, a search among the Chancery records will probably reveal the result, but it is improbable that the Company reaped any benefit from their action. And so she passes from the scene, a curious example of the vicissitudes to which Englishwomen in India were exposed.

Bibliography

Biddulph, Col. John. *The Pirates of Malabar and An English-woman in India Two Hundred Years Ago*. Londin, Smith, Elder & Co., 1907

Cordingly, David. *Under the Black Flag: The Romance and Reality of Life Among the Pirates*. New York, Random House, 1996.

Gosse, Philip. *The History of Piracy*. London, Longmans, Green and Co., 1932

Johnson, Capt. Charles. *A General History of the Robberies & Murders of the Most Notorious Pirates*, London 1724. This book has been reprinted many times. This book draws, in part, on accounts recorded in a 2002 edition by Conway Maritime Press in London.

Pirates Own Book: Authentic Narratives of the Most Celebrated Sea Robbers. Salem, Massachusetts. Marine Research Society, 1924. Reprint of a book first compiled by Charles Ellms in 1837.